THE MUSIC HUSTLE

THE MUSIC HUSTLE

HOW TO BOOK THE GIG

ANDY PENK

NEW DEGREE PRESS
COPYRIGHT © 2021 ANDY PENK
All rights reserved.

THE MUSIC HUSTLE
How to Book the Gig

ISBN   978-1-63676-377-4   *Paperback*
               978-1-63676-452-8   *Kindle Ebook*
               978-1-63676-378-1   *Ebook*

To my mom, dad, and grandfather, who have loved and supported me each day, and to Paul French and Paul Little, whom without I would have no story to tell.

CONTENTS

INTRODUCTION		9
CHAPTER 1.	WHO IS THE "MUSIC YOU"?	17
CHAPTER 2.	HAVE YOU PRACTICED LATELY?	29
CHAPTER 3.	SHOULD I KNOW THAT SONG?	39
CHAPTER 4.	WHY SHOULD I GO TO AN OPEN MIC NIGHT?	51
CHAPTER 5.	WHAT'S THE DEAL WITH THE SOUND?	71
CHAPTER 6.	WHY DOES AMBITION FEEL LIKE REJECTION?	77
CHAPTER 7.	HOW DO I ENGAGE MY AUDIENCE?	85
CHAPTER 8.	SHOULD I HAVE MAJORED IN MARKETING?	93
CHAPTER 9.	WHERE CAN I PLAY MY ORIGINAL SONGS?	103
CHAPTER 10.	SO IS THIS A COMPETITION?	113
CONCLUSION		119
ACKNOWLEDGMENTS		123

INTRODUCTION

It was the spring of 2015, and I was in a band that wasn't going to last much longer.

We were immature high school kids, and we all thought we were hot stuff. Yeah, we were good, but certainly not the greatest thing since sliced bread. We had a solid run for a high school group, playing some fun open mics, a school talent show, and a couple of performances in a local "Battle of the Bands" type of competition, in which we made it to the final round. However, it was extremely obvious we were going to implode as a group. Arrogance was running high among us; we didn't act like a team, as each of us wanted to show off that he was the better member of the group, and we certainly didn't look like a team on stage. Each member tried to get as much attention as possible. It was all very petty, to say the least.

Yet, acting like our band wasn't on a high-speed train toward certain doom—and during what ended up being the last month or so of us playing together—egos were running high, and we were looking to book gigs. We had no idea what we were doing. We sent a lot of places e-mails, and we wouldn't hear back. Friends and family would say they have an "in" with a manager at a venue, but nothing ever really came of these remarks. We'd show up at places and get weird looks when we said we wanted to play music there. We were failing and didn't know what we were doing wrong.

In the end, we only ended up getting one gig thanks to the parent of a band member. Ironically, after exerting so much effort trying to book a show, we broke up essentially right after we got this gig.

This brings us to the summer I thought about quitting music. Even though all of the band drama had stressed me out, I did love playing with my bandmates. They were all extremely talented musicians, and I consider myself lucky to have had the opportunity to play with them. That was part of why my mood was down; I didn't think I would ever play with such talented people again. The dream of being in a rock band was dying in front of my high schooler eyes.

I was discouraged because I had spent so much time with the band trying to book gigs. I had convinced myself we were about to start playing shows for an audience and finally share our music with more people. To watch the band break apart while acknowledging we had no substantial success in booking gigs was a hard pill to swallow. The thought echoed in my head: *If the five of us couldn't book a show without a parent knowing somebody who was booking, how was I going to ever book a show for myself?* My answer was simply that I couldn't and that was that. I had had no experience in the local music scene and had no connections of which to take advantage. I retreated to simply playing guitar in my basement.

God bless my mother, though. She—the saint of a woman she is—dragged me kicking and screaming out of my pity party. She told me she had found an open mic, we were going, and I was going to bring my guitar and play.

I said, "No."

She said, "Too bad."

Thus, I ended up in the car with my parents on our way to a run-down dive bar in Old Orchard Beach, Maine. I was upset and did not want to go. I just wanted to wallow in self-pity, left to believe I was not capable of succeeding. My mom knew I could succeed, though, and she forced me to take the first step to make myself believe I could succeed again.

While my mother was able to get me in the car, I did not bring my guitar. So, we ended up sitting at a table in this bar and just watching people perform. I sat there, listening and observing. I had only ever been to a couple of different open mics before and was trying to get a feel for how this one worked. Listening was hard though, as my parents pushed me to go sign my name on the sheet so I would be on the queue to play. As I hadn't brought my guitar, I wasn't quite sure how that would work, but I was invested in ending the harassment. So, I got up from my chair, put my name on the sheet, and sat back down at the table.

The prodding stopped, but the nerves shifted into high gear. I realized, beyond not having an instrument there, I had no idea what I was going to play when they called me up. I had only ever done an open mic with the band before, and I was just the singer. In other words, I knew the lyrics, but I had no clue how to play our songs on a guitar. Yes, I knew how to play other songs, but I had never really played much from memory, especially not in front of an audience.

After about twenty long minutes, I was called up to the stage. The host of the open mic handed me his wonky, out of tune guitar, and I just played the first song that came to mind that I might know all of the lyrics to—U2's "With or Without You." I finished and got a lot of applause, which made me feel really good. I had never walked into a place before, played a song, and received such great reception, knowing no one there but my parents. It gave me a sense of affirmation about myself as a musician I had never gotten before.

I ended up playing one more song—Bon Jovi's "Wanted Dead or Alive"—and it really got the people at the bar singing along. I gave the guitar back to the open mic host and headed toward my table. On the way, I was stopped by two gentlemen who told me they really liked my sound and invited me to an open mic they hosted at another bar across the street the following night. I ended up going the next evening and every week after that. In fact, that opportunity led to my first paying gigs.

I tell this story because I see it as the start of my professional career as a musician. It started with a sense of defeat and the belief I was never going to make it anywhere with music, but with a little support, it ends with me putting myself out there and proving I could have success with a musical career. On that night at the open mic, a door opened which led me to all the musical opportunities that came after.

From my experience, most people unfamiliar with booking gigs think it is a rather easy thing to do, assuming if one has the talent, they can easily be paid to play wherever they want. The problem with this view is it disregards the importance of building a network of contacts in the industry and the making of a good musical reputation, or a musical resumé. Instead, it favors viewing musical talent as the only important feature. Time and effort are needed to attain a network and a positive reputation, and then gigs may be booked successfully and consistently.

By no means have I had an illustrious, high-profile musical career. I am a college student who has spent most of my life playing music in some capacity. Over the past six years, I have been playing gigs at bars and restaurants around Portland, Maine. More importantly, I have been able to earn money consistently by playing music at bar and restaurant gigs. The idea for writing this book came about from musical friends who have asked me how I got myself into the position of being able to earn money playing music. I aim to help them, as well as the many talented musicians who busk or gig without consistency, who could be successful if they learned the best practices for booking gigs. Further, the inspiration for this book also came during the coronavirus pandemic, in which seemingly endless masses of musical people posted videos of themselves playing music. Many of these folks are extremely talented and have the potential to be able to perform live once the pandemic concludes. I hope reading this book will help offer these people the knowledge base to professionally perform and pursue their musical passions, as well as attain the accompanying financial profit from gigging.

In this book, I hope to pass along my knowledge of booking gigs as well as share with you insights from gigging musicians and others in the industry from across the country. In the process of writing this book, I have interviewed musicians from Boston, New York City, Cleveland, my native city of Portland, and more. I have also interviewed venue owners for their perspectives on hiring talent, and I've talked with some folks who work at record labels and music agencies for their insights regarding how one can best market their music.

From my experience and conversations with others, there is not a one-size-fits-all approach to booking gigs. The "music you" is a term I use throughout the book, which I will define in-depth in the first chapter, but for now, you can think about it as the definition of yourself as an artist, which will impact how you specifically go about booking gigs. Once you understand yourself as an artist, you must be practiced, professional, and prepared. Further, you need to network well, support others, and if you are halfway decent, you should find success.

Ideally, this book is meant to be a guide for musicians who are looking to start gigging or looking to get more gigs. That said, I certainly think others could read it and take something away from it. If you are a parent of a musically inclined child, this may be an interesting read for you, as it may introduce you to the possibility of your child performing music at local venues as a part-time or summer job. And if you are not musically inclined but love music, this book will walk you through, step by step, how the musicians you see performing at your local live music venues secured the opportunity to perform there.

To my knowledge, there is not another book quite like this for musicians. If you stick with me through this book, I'll do my best to guide you along the journey to securing the gigs you want and understanding the process of booking gigs to ensure consistent bookings in the long term. I truly hope you enjoy the journey and apply the insights within for your benefit!

CHAPTER 1

WHO IS THE "MUSIC YOU"?

After I booked my first gig at the dive bar in Old Orchard Beach, Maine, I didn't suddenly know what I was doing. Yes, booking one gig made me feel like I could book more and motivated me to hustle to a variety of different places, but having gotten through the door at one place did not mean every other door was going to open up for me.

I thought about what a professional would do and then attempted to do it. I made a Facebook page that had a brief bio about who I was. I connected with someone to record a cheap demo CD to give to venue owners. I ordered some business cards to slip into the CD cases for when I gave them to the venue owners or restaurant managers I spoke with when attempting to book. Doing these things in an uninformed manner didn't help me.

Now, having been gigging for about six years, I know the ins and outs of the process: how to present myself, what to say to a booker, what information to have prepared for a booker, etc. I have played hundreds of gigs, and I have a network of musicians from across the country who have been playing gigs much longer than me, who I have since discussed with the best practices for successfully scoring gigs. But back then, I lacked a clear strategy. I did not have much of a pitch to present to venue owners. Aside from the general notion of offering live music, I did not have an in-depth understanding of what exactly I was offering and what my value was to the venues.

For example, and this is jumping ahead a little bit, when I got my first gig, I did not know enough songs to fill the requested three-hour time slot, and I did not have a lot of time to learn a ton of songs. So, I just started googling chords of songs I was familiar with—the genre and the decades in which the songs were released were irrelevant—and learned around forty seemingly random songs. The gig did end up going well enough and led to more gigs at this bar, but it easily could not have. Playing a ton of unfitting songs together, I had no discernible genre or style. Beyond that, I failed to consider what kind of music folks at a dive bar would care to listen to on a Saturday night.

These two components—defining one's style and understanding one's audience—help constitute what I will call one's musical self, or as I will refer to it from here on out, one's "music you." To understand the "music you," you need to answer the questions surrounding who you are as an artist. What is your genre? What is the audience you appeal to? And likely, the most crucial question for you as an individual is:

what is your motivation for wanting to perform live music? Let's take some time to break down each of these questions.

Determining your genre may seem like an easy first step; however, I would contend most people who want to play live music may need to think a bit harder about it. As a musician, you may already have a genre you like to play. Maybe it's jazz, or maybe it's rock. Maybe it's rap, or maybe it's pop. Maybe you like playing stuff from a variety of genres. Regardless, the first step is being honest about the kind of music you like and want to play, as you may find more opportunities to play specific genres over other genres.

Let's say, hypothetically, you live in a town with only rock and roll clubs, and you are a classical pianist. Would you be willing to play rock and roll music instead of your preferred classical music so you could perform? There are probably few cities and towns that only have venues that facilitate one music genre. Still, my example presents the reality that you will have more opportunities to play music if you are willing to play other genres aside from the ones you personally like the most. In my experience, I have found more venues facilitate the performance of mainstream genres—pop, rock, and country—than other genres like jazz, blues, and metal. That is not to say that if you are not playing pop, rock, and country you won't have the opportunity to play your music for an audience. I only mean you may not have as much opportunity to perform as a musician playing in the more mainstream genres.

So, the question you need to ask yourself is: am I willing to play another music genre for more opportunity to perform?

I can't answer that question for you. Only you know whether you will be happy playing a music genre that may or may not be your preference and having that genre be all or a part of your brand.

I would be remiss not to note there are plenty of musicians who are juggling different projects. By doing so, these musicians ensure they stay happy playing what they want while also dabbling in other styles they may not be as interested in so they can perform more. However, if you use this strategy, my suggestion is one of your projects be a band so if you are a solo artist in your other musical venture, there is a clear distinction of the difference between your two projects. The next step is to establish a clear expectation of what your audience can anticipate hearing from each project.

For example, Edgardo Cora, a professional drummer in the Greater Cleveland area, performs in a multitude of bands. Each of these projects is relatively different from one another. One is a blues group, while another is a jazz trio. He also plays in a pop-rock band. While he may gain the most personal enjoyment from playing in his jazz group, he plays in a variety of different groups with varying genres because, at the end of the day, he really just loves to play drums and make music for people to enjoy with his bandmates. His "music you" isn't defined by being a jazz drummer exclusively; his "music you" is being a drummer who is open to any and all musical opportunities that present themselves, regardless of the genres to which they pertain.

Moreover, it helps to consider the audience you are playing for, particularly concerning the genre or genres you have decided to align with the "music you." People have different musical preferences, and the places they frequent largely determine the type of music you would hear there. For example, if you go to a dive bar, chances are you aren't going to hear smooth jazz. Or, if you go to a jazz club, you're not going to hear someone playing Today's Top 40. There are two lessons here. First, think like you are your audience. Find out where the people who like your music are and hustle to get in the door. Second, don't force yourself through a door where your audience isn't. In other words, if you want to play at a particular venue but the audience isn't comprised of people who like the music you play, stop trying to get in the door and look for other, more appropriate places for the "music you." You will not find success playing for people who do not want to listen to you, so find the people who will.

Let's engage in another hypothetical situation to illustrate putting yourself in your audience's shoes: Let's say you are a singer-songwriter, playing exclusively original material. You have never played in front of a live audience before. One of the important questions you should ask would be: are there venues in your area that facilitate original music? If you google this, the results will likely show you large theaters that tend to host up-and-coming and/or established touring musicians. You may be a great musician, but don't flatter yourself into thinking a booking agent at these places would take you seriously yet. Remember, you have never played a gig before. Instead, you should put yourself in the shoes of your audience and question: where would they go to hear live music that is different from what they'd hear from the typical cover artists? Typically, the answer would be at open mics or coffeehouses. Playing at an open mic or a coffeehouse connects you with people who already like live music. It allows you to perform your original songs and get real feedback from new listeners, who may become new fans. I'll discuss open mics in much more depth in Chapter 4, "Why Should I Go to an Open Mic Night?" Open mics are a great way to both expose your music to new audiences and get yourself through the door to play music at a new venue.

Once you know your genre and who your audience is, you have almost finished defining your "music you." The remaining component is your motivation, the "why" behind why you want to perform. Is it because you love to share your musical talents with those around you? Is it because you are looking to monetize your talent? Is it a bit of both? Answering the question of motivation will determine some of the actions you may or may not be willing to do when hustling for gigs. Let's say your primary motivation is monetary gain. Would you be willing to play a pro bono gig at a venue to get in the door? Or would you be willing to play a gig at a venue that doesn't pay its live musicians apart from a tip jar? Maybe you would be willing to play a pro bono gig as an opportunity to potentially expand your audience. Motivation is a deeply personal matter, especially when it comes to one's finances, so these are decisions you have to make.

Alternatively, let's say your primary motivation is a passion for playing live. What if you need money at some point, but you have already established with all of the venues you play at that your talent isn't worth paying for (by never asking for payment or an established willingness to play pro bono)? Maybe some venue owners will look kindly upon your request, but others very well may not. Again, it is up to you how you want to position yourself as far as the monetary side of gigging goes. If you don't care if you get paid, that's your decision. If you do want to get paid, again, that's your decision. The choice is yours to make.

I would add, however, there is certainly nothing wrong with playing music for monetary gain. If you are good at playing music and someone wants to pay you for it, there is nothing wrong with that. As a college student, playing live music at bars and restaurants on weekends helped pay my student loans. I know there are music purists who contend musicians should only play out of passion rather than for money. They are more than welcome to hold that view. I am saying you should not feel like wanting or needing the money playing live music provides is bad; moreover, you should not feel like a disingenuous musician if that passion for performing isn't your primary motivator. You probably have bills to pay, so you shouldn't feel bad about playing music to pay them, even if someone else doesn't like it.

Having defined your genre(s), audience, and motivation, you now know your "music you" and are closer to beginning your hustle to book gigs and perform. However, before I close out this chapter, I would like to add some final advice—directed mainly toward musicians looking to play centrally at bars and restaurants—about connecting genre, audience, and motivation.

From my own experience performing at bars and restaurants, I've learned playing songs people know is typically the best way to keep playing at the venues you are established at and get on the books at more venues. People tend to like what they recognize and often stick around after eating or drinking if they recognize the songs and like your sound. Although you may have great original material, it is unfamiliar to your audience. Unfamiliar songs tend to make the audience disinterested, often causing them to leave venues that are not recognized or branded as overtly music-oriented. In contrast to bars and restaurants, music-oriented venues—such as coffeehouses or music clubs—host live music with great frequency, with audiences typically looking favorably upon unfamiliar music, and consistently feature artists who don't play covers in favor of originality.

Yes, I am suggesting if you want to maximize your profitability on the bar/restaurant level, you should "sell out" to some extent. I know that may be controversial to say, but please stick with me. That does not mean you should never play your original music. It just means if you want more gigs, you should know many songs people know and play at places where people want to hear covers, like bars and restaurants. That doesn't mean you also can't play where your original music is appreciated; you just need to find your balance for what you can tolerate artistically and financially. Most importantly, don't pigeonhole yourself. It's hard to rebrand yourself once you become either the "cover guy" or the "all original songs guy."

The final point I will raise is the advantages and disadvantages of playing in a band, as they significantly affect motivations. There are benefits to being a solo artist. As an individual, you will typically earn more than what you would make as a band member, and when booking, you don't need to wait to consult with everyone's schedules. Also, space in the venue is less of a factor to consider as a solo artist; you don't have to worry about how much room you need to set up a PA system, amps, drums, and the rest of your equipment. Additionally, you don't have to deal with drama from other bandmates, and the decision of what genre and songs you play is solely yours.

As far as disadvantages go, you may find some venues prefer a live band's cohesive sound. You may also find when you cover certain songs, they feel empty without some of the other instrumentation that is filled in by a band. Additionally, not being in a band puts all of the responsibility to book gigs and perform on you alone.

If you are in a band, that's fine too. Some advantages include getting to spend time performing and practicing with other talented musicians. You also get to enjoy a full sound you could never get when singing and playing guitar or piano alone. I played in a band for years and enjoyed it thoroughly. We played a lot of songs that would not have sounded as good with just me and my guitar. That said, it was logistically much simpler to do my own acoustic venture, so I left the band and have done well for the past few years. That was my personal decision.

Gigging by yourself may not be the right decision for you, as you may love the camaraderie that can come with a band. I don't mean to sway you one way or the other because at the end of the day, you can do both—having your own solo project and playing in a band. I only ask you to consider the pros and cons of each path, as it can be hard to build back your brand recognition if you decide to either a) leave a band you're established with and start a solo career or b) move from a solo career with local recognition to a band no one recognizes.

Option B is the more ideal scenario of the two, as bookers may be more inclined to give your band the opportunity to perform since they already like you, assuming you are the front person of the band. Option A may be more intimidating for them to book you, as they know the audience likes the band and they don't know whether a switch to acoustic will be too much of a change of pace or if you can even carry a gig on your own.

If you choose to play in a band, it is essential to know your motivation. Is your goal to earn money? Do you play an instrument that makes you relatively dependent upon other musicians to perform live? (Namely, do you play drums or bass? Or do you play guitar but don't also sing? Your ability to get a gig is essentially dependent on whether or not you are able to form a band.) Do you enjoy playing with your fellow bandmates a lot? If you can find out what your bandmates' answers are to these questions that would also be useful information. If you don't know what you and your bandmates' motivations are for playing in a band, it is much easier for the musical unit to lose cohesion and fall apart, leaving you without the group you love to play with or the income stream for which you may have joined the group.

While I genuinely enjoy playing with easygoing musicians, I have found the music hustle is much easier to pursue as a solo artist. Frankly, there's generally more money to be made on the bar and restaurant level playing solo. You also aren't dependent on your bandmates' potentially changing attitudes and motivations; thus, your income stream is not jeopardized. Lastly, it's just way easier to book gigs since you don't need to message and wait to hear back from each member every time you try to book a show. My bias is obviously toward playing acoustic solo gigs, but you don't need to take my personal preference as gospel. Decide for yourself what you want to do based on your own "music you."

Now that I have covered these final points regarding bar and restaurant musicians, I hope you now have a better understanding of your "music you" and that you are ready to continue learning the music hustle.

CHAPTER 2

HAVE YOU PRACTICED LATELY?

Let's be real for a minute. There are plenty of incredible musicians out there shredding up and down the neck of a guitar with ease, displaying stellar mastery of vocal cords, and knowing music theory like the back of their hands. An example of such stellar musicianship is my friend Darren Thiboutot. He's been playing guitar since he was ten years old. Before we met, he was playing guitar in his father's blues band and had even shared the stage with blues legend Buddy Guy. Darren is a phenomenal guitarist with a true mastery of fretboard, having spent years listening to blues records and not only learning how to play them but also learning how to connect to the soul of the blues. Many call him a guitar prodigy, and he has since gone on to open for Buddy Guy on more occasions and tour up and down the East Coast with his blues band Memphis Lightning, located in Florida.

I mention Darren as one of many extremely talented artists who exist at the type of venues in which you may want to play. He's the kind of artist who takes the time to practice more than he needs to in order to perform well, and he, or someone like him, is also potentially your competition when trying to book a gig.

To be clear, I myself am by no means a prodigy; I should honestly be a way better guitarist for the number of years I have been playing. That said, I practice in order to make sure I do not bomb when I perform for a crowd. Because if I did bomb, I would likely lose the gig and another musician would replace me

You've probably heard this plenty of times before, likely in other aspects of your life, but you are a small fish in a big sea. No matter how talented you are and no matter how much time you practice, there will always be someone better than you. That is not meant to discourage you from practicing because you will never be the best. I mean just the opposite; you should practice so you can be the best musician you want to be for what you want to do musically.

To offer an example of what I mean, I sing and play guitar at local restaurants. Playing at these venues is largely my end goal. I practice so I am able to play my music for the maximum enjoyment of my audience. I don't need to be as good of a guitarist as Eddie Van Halen to play acoustic guitar chords, nor as good of a singer as Andrea Bocelli to sing contemporary pop covers. Both of those artists are musicians "competing" in leagues far outside of my local establishment level.

I know the "music me" (and after reading Chapter 1, "Who Is the 'Music You'?" so should you), so I know who I am competing with for gigs: the musicians playing at the venues that best suit the "music me" and myself. Even when you get to the point where you excel at the musical capability you need to be at to be the "music you," that doesn't mean you should ever stop pushing yourself to be a better musician. I personally think that goes for anything in life. If you can be better at anything, why not put in the time and effort to do so?

If you read this and you are intimidated, don't fret (music pun intended). This is not a book about learning how to play music. It is a book about succeeding at scoring gigs, but success won't be found if you aren't good enough. It's harsh but a truth, nonetheless. I would like my readers to succeed, so I want to discuss some practice methods and services you may consider to help you improve your craft.

MUSIC LESSONS & YOUTUBE TUTORIALS

First and foremost, if you can afford lessons, I suggest taking them. There is a lot to be learned from a music teacher who has been playing for most of their life. Moreover, I think the central appeal of music lessons would be to learn theory. Having an adequate understanding of music theory makes both soloing and playing with a band significantly easier. Chords and scales stop being shapes and patterns; instead, they become a system that, once understood, opens a piece of music up to more creativity and/or improvisation.

If you plan on soloing at a gig, I highly recommend making sure you have a basic understanding of music theory. Knowing how the notes relate to one another will make a world of difference in your solos. According to my musical colleagues, an hour lesson may typically range between forty and sixty dollars, depending on the experience of the instructor.

This next piece of advice may not seem like it will be super helpful at first, but it has helped me out a lot when trying to learn songs quickly—YouTube. Honestly, the guitar tutorials I have found on this site are typically very helpful in both learning chords and specific songs. Marty Music is one of my go-to accounts for guitar tutorials. The guitar and piano tutorials on YouTube typically show the chords of a song and their shapes, and they are usually spot-on or at least mostly accurate.

While they tend to be aimed toward the beginner musician, if you are in a hurry to learn a certain lick in a song or just generally learn a song you aren't familiar with, YouTube videos are definitely worth checking out. There are also YouTube videos that explain theory if you can't or aren't willing to pay for lessons. While some videos can be rather lacking or altogether unhelpful, the majority of them are very useful in my experience—clearly demonstrating how to play the parts of a song or a certain scale.

APPS & PRODUCTS TO CONSIDER

In regard to practicing itself, practice with a metronome. I know it's obnoxious. *Tick tick tick tick*…seemingly droning on forever. As piercing as the sound is to the eardrums, it will truly help you play more in time. More importantly, if you practice with it enough, it will help you play in time with consistency. If you do not want to buy a metronome, there are plenty of free metronome apps you can download on your phone or computer.

However, if you are determined to avoid practicing with a metronome and you are practicing a specific song, I suggest downloading iRehearse 2. It is an app you can download to your computer that you can upload a song to, and it allows you to change the tempo of the song. If you are trying to learn a difficult song, it is always a good idea to take it slow. If you try to play it fast right away and keep messing up, you are creating muscle memory for your fingers on how to play the song incorrectly. If you slow the song down when you practice, you will master it at a slower pace and then you can steadily increase the tempo and have mastery of the song at any speed.

Another neat feature of iRehearse 2 is it lets you change the pitch of the song, so you can practice along with a recording if you want to play a song in a different key than the one in which it was recorded. This is certainly a beneficial feature for singers who may change the keys of songs often to make sure the vocal notes stay in their range comfortably. Currently, iRehearse 2 is listed at $11.99 on the App Store, so it unfortunately does cost money, but it is certainly a worthwhile investment to improve one's musicianship. It is also available on Android.

This next tool is specifically for singers, and I think it is extremely helpful. It is a product called HearFones. It's essentially a funky looking headset that has curved plastic extending from the earpieces to your mouth that catches the sound of your voice when you sing, letting you hear what you actually sound like instead of how you think you sound. Valued at forty dollars, they are a little pricy, but if you really want to work on your vocals, ensuring your tone is good and your singing isn't pitchy, HearFones are definitely a worthwhile practice tool.

Lastly, as far as technique is concerned for any instrumentalist, it is important to know your scales so that you can improvise well in any key that you are playing. For musicians in bands that need to play solos—whether they be played on guitar, piano, or another instrument—practicing your scales is of the utmost importance. If you don't, chances are that your solos will be poor and the audience will be aware that they lacked quality. Consequently, they may leave, which makes you look even worse in the eyes of the employees or managers watching their customers hurriedly exit the establishment. To avoid such an unfortunate result, I recommend practicing your scales with a metronome. Being able to play your scales at slower tempos creates strong muscle memory and makes playing scales at faster tempos much easier, which is beneficial for soloing.

WHAT I LIKE TO PLAY VS. WHAT I DON'T LIKE TO PLAY
Apart from the specific things I have mentioned that assist with practicing, it is also important to regiment your practice time. If you're being honest with yourself and know you need to improve to achieve your vision of the "music you," you need to have a planned practice schedule. Sitting down to practice every once and awhile, quite frankly, isn't going to cut it. Use a planner or calendar and mark down the times when you are going to practice. Improvement demands

consistency. Thus, if you aren't consistent with your practicing, your skill will not improve.

Moreover, when practicing, I like to think of that time as having two components: "what I like to play" and "what I don't like to play." Whenever I sit down to practice, I always start by playing whatever I need to improve on first. It could be a new piece or it could be a new scale, but they are the things I typically don't enjoy in the moment, as they introduce challenges. They can be hard to pick up without time and effort practicing them, so it is important not to be intimidated by new songs or scales, as learning them will both make you a better player and feel good about overcoming the challenge. Failing to practice things that are not challenging to you will result in your level of musicianship stagnating or possibly even getting worse. If you are not motivated to improve, you certainly won't become a better musician.

After I play "what I don't like to play," I switch gears to "what I like to play," or in other words, things I already know how to play. Typically, the things I already know how to play are songs I really like and are what drive a lot of my passion to play music to begin with. It is important to make time to play the things you already know how to play because—apart from these songs likely being the ones you are most passionate about—playing them will help you feel motivated to play the songs that are challenging for you now.

Think about it: every song you can play easily now was once a song that took you time and effort to master. Thus, every song you love to play now is a testament to the hard work you have put into becoming a better musician. It is in this part of your practice when you play what you are passionate about and remind yourself you've overcome obstacles in learning new music before.

As far as learning new songs go, one may wonder what the best way to go about this. As mentioned earlier, YouTube can be rather helpful in finding chords to learn songs and finding notes or tabs for riffs. Another site I find to be helpful is Ultimate Guitar. It is a fast and easy way to access the chords in a song, and there is a feature that allows you to change the key so if you are singing and playing, you can play the song in a key that is comfortable for your voice. The chords may not be perfectly accurate 100 percent of the time, but it is certainly a good starting point for learning a new tune. Chordify is another useful site for finding chords, as it shows you the changing chord shapes on the guitar neck along with the audio of the song.

***

This is as far as I want to go with discussing different practice tools and methods available for musicians. As I said earlier, this is not a book about learning how to play music, but about how to secure gigs. That said, this is all important information, especially for those reading who have not been playing an instrument for a significant period of time or aren't where they should be musically due to a lack of practice.

I do not mean to come across as someone with all of the answers. The techniques, tips, and products I have listed are all just things I have found useful in becoming a better musician. Maybe you won't find them useful or don't think you need them; that's fine. I put them here for those who could use some more help becoming a performance-level musician.

If you feel unprepared as a musician to start trying to book gigs, there was a time when I was certainly in your shoes. In fact, my first gig didn't go as well as it could have, in large part because I was unprepared. I had booked the gig a couple weeks before, and I did not know nearly enough songs to fill three hours. I had no idea how many songs I needed or how to learn them that quickly. I ended up at the gig without enough songs to play, so I began repeating songs when I saw the crowd turning over. Some of the songs I had put together didn't even suit my voice or genre. (Thankfully, most of the people were too drunk to notice I wasn't all that great.)

From a musical standpoint, it did not go well, but it was a great learning experience. Going forward, I knew I needed to find resources to help me learn songs and to spend more time practicing. I needed to make sure I was a professional and had a great setlist that suited me well. Now you know what I did to improve and make sure I was prepared for all of the gigs that came after.

Before turning the page to the next chapter and diving deep into the topic of making a great setlist, please be honest with yourself. If you know you aren't good enough to start performing now, that's alright, as long as you admit you need to practice to get better. You don't want to show up to your first gig and bomb like I did because first impressions matter. If you make a poor first impression, the door to playing at a venue may lock forever.

CHAPTER 3

SHOULD I KNOW THAT SONG?

Have you ever gone out to hear live music and found that, while you enjoyed the performance, the musical experience left something to be desired? Maybe it was just an off night for the artist, and they messed up some notes or chords. I think what is more likely to occur is the setlist is not up to par, lacking awareness of its appropriateness to a respective venue and/or audience.

I had such an experience in the fall of 2020. I had just booked a gig at a new venue in downtown Portland, Maine, along the waterfront. The place was a nice outdoor spot with a makeshift stage and a tent for live music, plenty of picnic tables, a food truck, and a bar. To me, the venue screamed reggae vibes or summer songs, maybe even an acoustic Jack Johnson vibe. What it most certainly was not was a place to play classic rock deep cuts, the songs off albums most people wouldn't know unless they were fans of the artist—which is exactly what I heard when I went to scope the place out prior to my first gig.

As far as best practices go when booking a gig, scoping out the venue is certainly one of them. It gives you the answers to nearly any question you may have. How much room do I have to set up my equipment? Is the load in (physically moving the equipment into the venue) going to be difficult? What is the appropriate volume for this venue? These are all important questions that are easily answered by going to the venue before your gig to see how other artists are set up. However, for the sake of this chapter, these are not the questions I will be focusing on. Instead, I will be addressing more foundational questions that can be asked once you know the "music you" and are well-rehearsed with your instrument. You are at a point where you know you can play a gig and are considering what venues you may want to play at. At this point, you should be asking these two questions: What songs would people like to hear at a particular venue? And what songs are other musicians playing at this venue?

When I entered the venue in Portland, I saw a five-man band and I headed to the back, just to stand there and listen to them. As a group, they played in time and, overall, they sounded quite good. The problem was I only recognized one song they played for the half hour I dropped in to listen. Granted, it was a band of older guys and I am in my early twenties. However, I do pride myself on being familiar with music from outside of my decade, especially sixties, seventies, and eighties music. And I wasn't the only one who didn't recognize their songs. The easy way to tell whether people like your song selection is to listen for the applause. There are generally two reasons an audience will not clap after a song. The first is you don't sound good, and I would refer you to reread the previous chapter about practicing if you have this problem. The second is they either do not know the songs you are playing or do not like the songs you are playing. In this venue, the majority of people there were folks in their thirties, and they were not clapping. As I previously said, the band sounded good; their fault was their setlist left much to be desired.

To improve their setlist, this band should have started by considering what their audience at a particular venue wanted to hear. Notice that I said a particular venue and not just at a venue. Setlists are generally not "one size fits all." If they were, it would imply you believe everyone at all of the places you play has exactly the same taste. I have found people tend not to be that monolithic in their musical preferences. Also, if you did assume you were playing for the same audience every night, a one size fits all setlist—a setlist you use for every gig at every venue—would bore your audience if they hear all the same songs every time you play. Thus, to best tailor your setlist to your audience, you need to go to your audience at the specific venue you want to play at and actually see what songs they like.

You probably already have a good idea of some of the venues that may suit your genre. Plan to go there on a night they have live music (call ahead or check their social media that day if you aren't sure). When you're there, you need to look around and listen intently. Note how the audience is reacting. Are they clapping, singing, and/or tapping their feet along? Note their demographic information; the most significant trait is usually their age. Observe the musician(s); note their song selection (actually write down every song they play); whether they play songs from a variety of genres or stick to one; and if they play with energy—that is, they look happy to be there and move around a little bit. Chances are this means the audience will display positive reactions.

Another important note that is often overlooked is observation of the waitstaff at the restaurant. Be aware of their reactions to the musician. Try to get a sense if they are happy with the music the artist provides because they regularly interact with the manager, who is often the booker. Oftentimes when I play a venue for the first time, someone from the waitstaff will approach me to offer a compliment about the music and say they'll ask the manager to have me play again. While the positive opinion of waitstaff may not guarantee you another gig on its own, a negative opinion will hurt you. This is because complaints about your music from people who are friendly, or more closely associated, with the manager tend to carry more weight in the decision of whether to rebook you. So if the live music you're observing sounds good but the people who work at the restaurant do not appear happy with it, it does not bode well for your ability to perform the same kind of music there.

If you have done a good job scoping out the venue, you should have a better understanding of how to make a setlist that is appropriate for that venue. I caution you not to ignore or dismiss any of your observations in favor of your own musical preferences. Please let that sink in. I repeat: do not dismiss the evidence you have compiled for how to make a great setlist for this venue in favor of whatever songs you may prefer to play. The reality of performing live music—much like life—is it is not about you. Your main focus is always pleasing your audience because that is how you get to play at a venue again. If the music you like to play is not the type of music an audience at a particular venue wants to hear, either find a venue where the audience would like to hear it or go play that music on your own time. Your setlist may be great, but if it does not assimilate to what the audience likes or is familiar with, you will fail. You can't force someone to enjoy eating food they don't like, just as you can't make someone enjoy listening to music they don't like.

Making a setlist is a topic I discussed at length when interviewing Edgardo Cora, an experienced drummer in the live music scene who plays in several local bands in the Greater Cleveland area. An important insight he offered was when making a setlist, the atmosphere may change at a particular venue from a Friday to Saturday. In other words, one should not just make a setlist they use all the time when playing at a certain venue. Instead, one needs to be cognizant of the different audiences that may be in attendance on different nights. For example, at a local restaurant, you may find the Friday night crowd consists of older folks while the Saturday night crowd is typically comprised of younger folks. These two groups will likely have different tastes in music and would probably not enjoy listening to the same songs. Thus, it would not be appropriate to play the same setlist for both crowds. You should make setlists tailored to the different audiences you expect to encounter.

Furthermore, the energy in the room is also something that needs to be considered. It may not seem like this is something that would impact a setlist significantly, but it certainly does. To offer an anecdote, in my first few months of gigging, I had an awful setlist. As I mentioned in the prior chapter, I had just hurriedly learned a bunch of random songs and prayed the gigs would go well. As I played each gig, I found there were songs that were always hits, but others were definitely duds. I took note of this and found the songs that went over the best were songs the audience was familiar with, meaning they could sing along, get rowdy, and raise the energy of the room.

I was playing at a dive bar with folks in their fifties and sixties, so these were songs like Jimmy Buffett's "Margaritaville" and Bon Jovi's "Wanted Dead or Alive." The songs that flopped were songs I really liked, but they did not fit in with the classic rock musical-leaning of my audience. These songs were a tad slower and also more modern, such as Ed Sheeran's "Thinking Out Loud" and Adele's "Rolling in the Deep." They tended to lose the audience's interest, lowering the engagement and overall energy of the room I had built up from playing songs they were familiar with.

Edgardo's advice in regard to setlists and maintaining the energy of the audience is to write preliminary setlists for the gig in pencil. After scoping out the venue on the weeknight you plan on performing, make a setlist based on the vibe you get from the audience. But, when you get to the gig, you should be willing to change the setlist as the night goes on if the energy of the room is not what you expect. Let's say you show up to play a Sunday brunch gig, expecting your audience to want to hear some mellow tunes, but then a large party barges into the venue to celebrate a special occasion.

Chances are the celebrating party is going to bring up the energy level in the room, and they will want to hear more upbeat tunes. You should be able to adapt your setlist on the fly to account for such a scenario.

To add a bit more to the conversation about forming a setlist in relation to an audience's energy and preferences, one may wonder what songs they should know. I'm not going to walk through every song I think an artist should know in accord with their respective genre. If you enjoy playing music in a certain genre and listen to it often, you probably have a good idea of which songs in the genre are the more famous. I highly recommend playing songs that are well-known to people. Less popular songs are by no means bad, and it isn't necessarily a gig-killer if you play a couple songs people don't know. That said, unless you are a singer-songwriter, a group playing original music, or maybe in the jazz genre, my general rule is almost every song you play should be a song people recognize.

I spoke with Darren Thiboutot, who said when he plays with his band, Memphis Lightning, they have a full list of all of the songs they know how to play that they bring with them to every gig. Simply having a list of songs is a great practice because if people ask for requests, you can provide them with the list and say, "This is what I know." Also, Darren organizes his list with columns for the key the songs are in, as well as the tempo. This is extra helpful because it allows the band to be more adaptable to their audience on the fly. If the energy in the room suddenly increases and they want to continue that high energy, he can just refer to the list and see what songs they have at a faster tempo. Since they also have the keys there, they can ensure they aren't playing too many songs, one after another, that sound too similar.

Chris Humphrey, a music educator and gigging musician from Maine, corroborated the effectiveness of preparing a list of songs by key and tempo. Differently, he also includes a column for style on his list. Primarily performing jazz music, he includes whether a song is classified as swing, cool jazz, Latin, or fusion. If you are a jazz musician, this could be a useful addition to your song list, again, ensuring not all of your songs sound the same. For non-jazz musicians, this can still be helpful because by being able to see all of the songs you know, arranged by style or genre, you can then determine if there are areas in which you may need to learn more songs in order to increase the variety you aim to offer.

Moreover, on a personal note, I love writing my own music, and performing my own tunes is the most rewarding musical experience for me. That said, I play almost exclusively covers at every gig. Covers reign supreme because, unless your audience is looking to be exposed to new music, you should assume your audience hates the unfamiliar. If they came out to the restaurant you're playing at because they saw a social media post from the joint saying they are having live music, chances are they did not turn out to hear songs they don't know if they'll like.

Thus, my advice would be as follows for original tunes and lesser-known songs: either leave them out or play one or two if it's a cover gig, separated in different sets. If you start playing multiple songs in a row people do not know, they will walk out, especially if they were already done with their meal and were just sticking around because they enjoyed the music. I cannot stress enough that unfamiliarity kills. In my first couple years of gigging, this was a big problem I had because I really liked playing my own songs. But, if I ever played two of my own songs back-to-back or two lesser-known covers one after the other, people just got up and left. You'd be surprised how fast a venue can go from being a full house to nearly barren.

Another consideration when making a setlist is tempo, specifically in regard to the ballad. I'm a sucker for a good ballad—a lot of people are. There's a reason Ed Sheeran and John Mayer got so popular; they both know how to write a damn good slow song. That said, I do not recommend stacking your setlists with ballads. They're rather low energy and can often be a hinderance to improving the vibe in the room, especially if you already had the energy level up with some faster songs. Furthermore, playing too many ballads can pigeonhole you into the reputation of being the "love song guy." If that's what your goal is, by all means go for it, but I think it is rather limiting. I've talked with restaurant owners and managers who have told me they have given artists the boot for constantly playing sappy, slow songs because it made their establishments feel dead. Ballads instill low energy; you aren't making people excited to stay and listen.

I don't recommend skipping playing ballads altogether, though. I would say one or two ballads per set, separated by a few songs, is appropriate. I always aim to have the most medium-paced songs on a setlist, then several fast-paced songs and a few ballads. I see this as a sort of middle ground tempo model that doesn't demand excessive high energy or minimal-to-no energy throughout the set.

Furthermore, one of the most important parts of composing a setlist is saving some really strong songs for the end. When I go out and hear live music, I typically find most artists end on a well-known song they perform very well. This is obviously what you should try to do, but the rest of the set preceding that last song of the night should not be dismissed. Remember, if you bore your audience, they will get up and go home. They do not owe you the privilege of playing for them. Thus, I recommend composing the last set with medium- and faster-paced songs to keep up the energy level in the room.

Plus, if people stay longer, typically that means they also drink more and thus make poorer financial decisions. What does that mean for you? It means the drunker your audience is, the more potential there is for you to make very good tips. This typically means you get tipped a twenty-dollar or ten-dollar bill instead of a five-dollar or one-dollar bill.

I would be remiss if I didn't mention I have been tipped with one-hundred-dollar bills before, simply for playing songs in my last set people could sing along to as they got more intoxicated. Obviously, there is no guarantee that increased tips will come your way, but adding familiar, upbeat songs in your last set is certainly something to consider implementing if you want to increase your odds of earning more, especially if monetary gain is pertinent to the "music you." This point once again speaks to how important it is to know the preferences of your audience and one should actually scout venues out before playing there in order to verify their assumptions about the audience, maximizing the chances of a successful gig.

Now, please allow me to backpedal a little bit. There are certainly occasions where it is appropriate to play original tunes. These circumstances would include your "music you" being defined as centrally a singer-songwriter and the venue you are performing at being welcome to and generally recognized as a place where artists play original material. When speaking with Lyle Divinsky, an accomplished musician who spent years hustling with his original songs in the music business in New York City, he said if an artist knows their audience came to the venue to see him/her play specifically, the artist can take more liberty with what songs are played.

Moreover, he offered an insightful analogy for how a musician can think of oneself when making a setlist: "You're a storyteller, gluing the whole scene together. What songs enhance the vibe and what ones push against it, creating a tension and push and pull in the set? You can bring in a weird song to push people's ears." In other words, when compiling and arranging songs to put in a setlist, songs that are unexpected or unfamiliar are not necessarily bad to play, so long as your audience is familiar with you and looking for you to engage their ears with the unfamiliar.

Since by now you have determined the "music you," you know your genre and the audience you should appeal to. In order to find this audience, you need to go to venues where you think the audience would like you and casually observe other people playing there to get a feel for the preferences of the audience. Once you have done that, you can start the process of formulating a setlist for a gig there. In the next chapter, we will discuss the importance of open mics and how they can help a musician build a reputation to get them gigs at their desired venues.

CHAPTER 4

WHY SHOULD I GO TO AN OPEN MIC NIGHT?

———

I opened this book by telling the story of my first open mic in Old Orchard Beach, Maine, in 2015. Performing at that open mic introduced me to musicians engaged in the local music scene who invited me to play at another open mic at a different venue. I attended that open mic nearly every week that summer. I built relationships with those musicians, and after consistently good performances, those musicians pushed the owner to ask to book me for dates on the venue's calendar.

So, for me, open mics were my central avenue into the world of gigging. That said, from my discussions with other musicians, it is not the only way. In fact, I would suggest there are five different major routes into the world of gigging: 1) open mics, 2) cold-calling and cold marketing, 3) playing for free, 4) utilizing connections in a previously established network, and 5) social media. Social media will be discussed in a later chapter because there is a lot that goes into using social media effectively.

OPEN MICS

I thought it would be fitting to speak with one of the open mic hosts who really helped jumpstart my musical career, a gentleman by the name of Michael Krapovicky. After attending the Old Orchard Beach open mic, I drove north and started attending an open mic at a restaurant in Lewiston, Maine, where Michael has been hosting for just under ten years. After attending his open mic a couple times and before I really had any "street cred," Michael would save me my preferred time slot on the open mic sign-up list (if I let him know I was coming ahead of time), and he also referred me to bookers of several venues who had offered him gigs he could not take due to scheduling conflicts. Between the gigs he referred me to and the gigs I got from restaurant owners and managers hearing me play at the open mic, my musical resumé grew considerably, which helped me obtain the opportunity to perform at new venues later.

At an open mic, you show up to the venue where it is hosted, prepared to play about five songs, although I find you will typically play only about three songs (that identify with the "music you"). When you play at an open mic, you are giving the venue a live sample of what you would play at a gig there; thus, you want the songs you play to be representative of your musical identity. These songs should be memorized, as it shows you are professional, well-rehearsed, and better enabled to connect with the audience. Since you won't be staring at your music stand, you can engage those in the room and really sell yourself as a performer and not just as a talented musician.

Additionally, I recommend bringing your own instrument and any cables you may need. You can typically borrow an instrument, and the cables to plug you into the sound system should already be there. But it never hurts to bring your own equipment in case there is an issue with their equipment or you do not feel comfortable playing the instrument you borrow.

Upon arriving at the venue, you should immediately put your name in the queue to perform so you hopefully do not have to wait too long to perform. While you wait, be respectful of the musicians who perform before you. Applaud their performances, even if they do not sound great; it is just the courteous thing to do. While you're waiting, if musicians are hanging around in the queue and chatting, it certainly wouldn't hurt to introduce yourself and network with them. You don't need to be best friends with them, but being acquaintances and building rapport could potentially help you down the line.

When it is your turn, you will be introduced, but it would not hurt to quickly introduce yourself again to make sure anyone who likes your performance knows your name and to start creating name recognition at the venue. Then you will tell the audience what song you are going to play, play the song, thank the audience, and repeat the cycle of introducing the song, playing the song, and thanking the audience until you finish your last tune. When you are done with your set, you will once again thank the audience for listening, repeat your name, and if you plan on playing at their open mic again the following week, tell them that. If you do this, people who like you may come back the following week to hear you again, and the venue will likely notice clientele returned to hear you.

When you leave the stage, if you can, stay around to hear at least a couple musicians play. Again, this is a courteous thing to do, as the other musicians at the end of the queue are likely being respectful, listening to you and everyone else ahead of them play.

When discussing both the expected and the potential benefits of performing at open mic nights, Michael offers some useful insights. For anyone who expects attending an open mic to help make them into the next big musical sensation, you're probably a little off-base. Michael sees open mics as a stepping-stone into the local scene, not a key to finding national success. For success on a national level, you generally have to search for somebody who has an "in" in the music industry. Then you would need to sort of be shopped there by a number of different folks at labels—most likely at a very young age. Moreover, to be discovered nowadays, Michael believes one needs a strong social media presence with videos that are glossy and slick, having one's musical identity very centered on what the label would be looking for. Further, the major music labels would likely not recognize open mics as substantial progress in one's musical career.

That said, Michael thinks a realistic expectation from attending open mics would be a musical career in general. From hustling at different open mics, one can work to start a career at a local, grassroots level. He asserts the local scene will always need musicians, and it gets easier and easier to put on a show that's very high quality, even with only one person.

He thinks the one-person show is changing; it's becoming less about guitar and a voice and more about the overall experience. With loops and different things that can alter your sound, one could almost be a DJ with a voice. Michael sees this as an especially cool part about open mics, as they let you show off how you are unique from other artists, tapping into the ways you can be different, even if it's just your voice and guitar.

And, apart from the aspect of creatively performing and the focus on differentiation—especially regarding the utilization of newer musical tools such as loopers—an open mic is a really quick way for somebody to sit down and just show off what they can do. One does not need to fully immerse themselves into new musical technologies if they don't want to. They can get up on stage and simply perform their music well, with no glitz and frills, and there are rewards to be had just by doing that and entertaining an audience.

Having hosted his open mic for as long as he has, Michael recognizes there are a lot of people who use it as a stepping-stone for work. They play at his open mic, are able to play a gig where the open mic is held, and then they can say that's one place they've already worked. Then they can grow the list of places they play at from there.

Not only does Michael see open mics as beneficial for the musicians looking to play there for gigs, he also sees open mics as beneficial to the venues where the open mics are held. If a musician sounds good; is professional, prepared, and attends repeatedly to show one can consistently perform well; is approachable, friendly, and courteous to the staff and other performing musicians; is able to engage the audience; and the audience enjoys the performance, the venue will notice. Most likely, the venue, after some time, will hire the musician because it notices its clientele enjoy a new artist featured during the open mic. The benefit of the open mic to the venue is the venue doesn't need to waste time looking for the talent, as the talent comes right to them.

For the bar and restaurant level, I think open mics are an extremely beneficial tool to get yourself into the gigging scene, from which you can then leverage yourself into new gigs at other venues.

COLD-CALLING & COLD MARKETING
Another strategy is cold-calling and cold marketing. Cold-calling refers to calling up a venue and asking if you can play there, and cold marketing refers to other means of pitching yourself to a venue, such as giving them a demo CD. Frankly, these tactics are not nearly as effective as open mics are, especially when you first start playing. Granted, not every venue has open mics, so some places rely on other means of getting in the door.

That said, a lot of the failure in cold-calling and marketing is not knowing who you need to contact. If you get the name of the owner, he/she may not be the person who handles booking. The manager may not be either. The task may be delegated to a bartender or another member of the venue's staff. Moreover, beyond the uncertainty of not knowing who to talk to, there is no guarantee if you are able to connect with them that they will call or e-mail you back to book or even listen to your demo CD. Unfortunately, this is a sentiment shared by every musician I interviewed for this book. The booking agent is typically busy with other responsibilities at the venue and will likely forget you called or just discard the CD you left.

I don't say this to discourage cold-calling and marketing. In fact, I have done a fair amount of cold marketing to get gigs. I bring up the downsides to illustrate it is not extremely effective and does not consistently yield results. For a few months in high school, at the end of many school days, I would drive around to different restaurants and bars to pitch myself to them and leave them with a demo CD. I only got a gig at one out of about ten of those establishments from that strategy. I would go in and follow up with the places I didn't hear back from, but it became apparent to me I was just being a nuisance to them, and I needed more street cred before I would be taken seriously, especially because I was so young at the time. However, over the next couple years, I secured gigs at nearly all of the places I hustled at, and this is how.

Once you have decided on a venue where you want to perform, figure out who the booking contact is. Typically, it will be the manager, but it may not be. Go onto the venue's website and either call or e-mail them to ask who does the booking at their establishment. For a call, say something along the lines of: "Hi, my name is X and I am a musician in the local area. I've seen other musicians play here who I think are stylistically similar to me, so I think I would be a good fit to perform here too. Could I please get the name and number or e-mail of the person who does the booking? And do you mind telling me what time they are usually there so

I can drop off a demo CD?" (You aren't really going to give them a CD, though. I'll explain that in a bit.)

Also, asking for the manager would be appropriate, as you know the manager will definitely know the answer to your question and may be the person who you want to talk to anyways.

Never, I repeat, *never* ask for the owner. Assume the owner is the busiest person at the business, and he/she is the last person you want to bother. Agitating the owner and burning a bridge with him/her is a surefire way to not get the gig—ever.

For an e-mail, a similar message would suffice, perhaps with a bit more about you as a musician. That said, I would not write an excessive bio about yourself and overwhelm the basic contact at the venue, especially when this general contact is not the person you need to win over. Hopefully, your call or e-mail is successful, and you will likely get the name of the person who does the booking, their contact information, and the times they are there.

Next, reach out to whoever the booking contact is, and be aware of the mindset the owner or manager may have—specifically if you are aiming to play at a bar or restaurant. This mindset in booking music is a problem. They do not know you, and thus, they do not know if you are good or if hiring you will bring more people to their venue who wouldn't be there otherwise. You need to win them over and convince them to give you a chance. I recommend calling the booking contact. He/She probably will not answer, so leave a voicemail briefly telling them who you are and that you are inquiring about potentially playing at their venue. I would then wait a couple days; if you don't hear back, send a follow-up e-mail. If you still don't receive a response after a few more days, I would then go to the venue in person at one of the times the person on the phone initially told you he/she would be there, and I would ask to speak with the booking contact.

Assuming whoever greets you at the entrance does not tell you the booking person is not present, you now get to speak in person with the booking contact, which is the most ideal situation to be in. However, it is your one and only chance to make a good impression with the person who can secure you the gig. In this interaction, the two most important things you can be are confident and professional. You should not be too confident so as to exude an air of arrogance, as that will certainly be off-putting to anybody. But you should be confident in your pitch.

When speaking with Dan Drouin, the owner of Stockhouse Restaurant and Sports Pub in Westbrook, Maine, he attested to the importance of a musician's pitch delivery. Specifically, he noted that for most of the musicians he books, they are both personable and professional in their delivery. When delivering your pitch, you should not be stumbling when telling him/her what type of music you play, where you've played previously, and what your repertoire is. You should have this down cold, otherwise you look like an amateur, and a venue isn't going to put their neck out for an amateur when more experienced musicians are knocking on their door.

Moreover, you need to be professional, recognizing this, in its essence, is a business transaction, especially to the venue.

While you may just want to perform because it is something you love to do, the venue will likely be paying you, and there is financial risk in hiring someone with whom they are unfamiliar.

Addressing the issue of unfamiliarity, this is where I stumbled in my early music hustling days. I did not have a list of places I had played before to share with the booking contact. I knew I was good enough to perform, but I did not have a reputation to prove it. Thus, this whole cold marketing strategy becomes significantly more effective once you have already gotten into the doors at other venues, as you can name-drop those venues when pitching yourself to new ones. I overcame this issue of unfamiliarity by playing at different open mics, getting gigs from people hearing me there, and then referencing those places I performed at in my pitches at the venues I wanted to perform at.

Thus, when talking to the booking contact, you will want to overcome this problem of unfamiliarity with a list of other places you have played. If you do not have that list, I would either pray the rest of your pitch is good enough for the booker to still consider you or wait until you have gotten yourself through the door of other venues by other methods, such as open mics. Along with a list of other places you have played, you should be able to tell them your repertoire—provide them with a bio and one or two samples of your music. These samples should ideally be videos of you performing so the booker gets an idea of who you are as a performer and what your sound is. The videos do not need to be professionally shot or mixed. They are just meant to provide the booking agent with an idea of who you are and what you are offering.

In my discussion with Edgardo Cora, he emphasized you should never give a booking contact a demo CD. This was certainly counter to the advice I had received when I started hustling, but it makes a lot of sense. Edgardo points out the booking agents are not your fans. They aren't going to take the time to sit down and listen to your CD. You may think they should be interested in listening to your CD so they can decide whether or not to book you. You're right, they should. But, as previously said, booking typically isn't their only job at the venue, and they have other things to do. Besides, CDs are steadily becoming obsolete. Sending them links to videos of you playing is way more convenient for them. Further, video clips are superior to demo CDs because it not only captures you performing, but it shows *where* you are performing. If you can give them video of you performing at a competing venue, it makes you considerably more desirable.

Assuming your pitch is well-received, the booker will ask you what is almost certainly the most important question to them: what is your rate? There are a few ways to answer this. You can undercut your value, offer a middle value, or overprice yourself. I highly recommend not overpricing yourself. If you ask for too much, the booker will know you're asking for more than they pay professionals in the booking circuit because he/she knows how much the venue pays everyone who plays there. Further, a big price tag is just a way for them to instantly stop considering hiring you. And I recommend always operating under the assumption people talk; if you say you've played at another place, it would not be surprising if the manager happens to know someone at that other place and calls their manager to ask if they like you and how much you charge there. If the number is way off, they will know you tried to screw them for more money. Being consistent with your rate is generally the best policy in my opinion.

Another way to price yourself is to undercut your own value. I see this as a dangerous strategy to some extent because it can potentially put you in a bit of a hole. Let's say you normally charge one hundred fifty dollars, but you really want to perform at this reputable venue, so you tell them you'll play for one hundred dollars. You are increasing the odds they will hire you, as you have made yourself more economically viable, but you have stated to them you are worth less than you really think you are. It is a challenge to increase your pay later on after doing this, as no employer particularly enjoys hearing their employee ask for a raise. If you want to avoid that conversation, undercutting your value is not the path for you. But, if you are going to undercut yourself, I suggest sticking with the lesser wage for at least a year before asking to raise your price.

I typically like to offer the going rate—whatever they pay other musicians who play there or what I am paid on average between different venues. The amount paid is a bit different in different markets. I recommend asking any gigging musicians you know what they get paid at different places. If you don't know any gigging musicians, counter the booker by asking what they usually pay. If it seems like a low-ball offer, ask if they would be willing to pay however much more. If they say no, take the gig if you are willing to play for what they offered. Otherwise, say, "Thank you for your time," and leave.

If the booker does not ask for your rate, the booker may look to have a cover charge for the night. In other words, the booker has patrons pay "X" amount at the door in order to cover the cost of the music. Sometimes a booker will offer the musician all of the cover charge; other times he/she will want to split the charge fifty-fifty or by another percentage. If the booker indeed wants to do a cover charge—especially if the cover charge is being split between you and the booker—instead of guaranteeing you payment outright, he/she will inquire as to how many people you can bring, as the number of people a band can bring directly affects the profits of the venue on a particular night. An alternative to this would be the booker offering you "X" percent of sales at the bar that night.

I personally prefer gigs where the booker and I agree to a set payment ahead of time that is not dependent on the number of people paying the cover charge or buying drinks. However, this alternative method of payment is something you may encounter at some venues, so it is important to be aware of this possibility and to be ready to negotiate your percentage of a cover charge if you have to.

Furthermore, I strongly recommend against playing for free to get in the door if you ever hope to make money from gigging. By telling a venue you will play for free, it does two things: 1) shows you are desperate and 2) values your musicality as not worth paying for. If you were to do this, it is undercutting your value to the most extreme degree you could. If you decided to ask for a raise later, it makes that conversation with the booker way harder, as you will be going from asking for nothing but the opportunity to perform to potentially upward of one hundred fifty dollars. And, when you ask for the raise, you will probably find they say "no" because they may have only hired you because you were free and not for your musical talent at all, which would be extremely disappointing and defeating. Thus, you should really aim to value yourself at what you think you are worth comparatively to competing musicians or just go with the average market rate.

PLAYING FOR FREE
That said, I do refer to playing for free as one of the common routes for booking gigs. I do this mainly because it was a piece of commonplace advice I received when I first started playing gigs. If you think about it from a practical level, the venue has essentially nothing to lose by having you play for free. So yes, you could likely get gigs this way pretty effectively if you just went around and offered to play for free everywhere. But, as I said previously, you will need to work yourself out of a big gap in expectations between you and the booker, who you've led to believe your music isn't worth anything.

From my perspective, the only times it makes sense to offer to play for free are for charity gigs and fundraisers or if you are truly desperate to play at a venue that will greatly bolster your musical resume. Playing for free at a more renowned venue should be able to open doors for you by allowing you to name-drop at other places. This name-drop should be able to help you secure more gigs in order to make up the money lost by pigeonholing yourself into playing at the well-known music spot for free. If playing for free is something you are willing to do, that is your prerogative. Just keep in mind although it can potentially be beneficial, it certainly comes with its downsides.

In the same vein of playing for free, I recommend not putting yourself in the position of playing for just tips. It's really playing with fire as to whether or not you will make any money at all. The venue's clientele just might not feel like tipping you, or maybe it was a bit chilly at your outdoor gig so fewer tipping individuals attended. That said, regardless of if you are being compensated or playing for free, it is generally appropriate to set up a tip jar at a restaurant or bar gig unless you are told explicitly not to do so by the venue's staff.

The tip jar should not be placed directly in front of you, so as not to hold the audience's attention while they are trying to watch you. Placing it directly in front of you may be construed as you begging for tips, so it is more appropriate for you to put the jar a bit to your side, with a sign placed in the jar that says "Tips." Also, you can potentially increase the amount of tips you get by seeding the tip jar with a few small bills before you start playing. If the jar is transparent, the audience may be more inclined to tip since they will see the money in the jar and think other people already have.

With all of this said regarding pricing, so long as your pitch is good and the booker finds your price manageable or appealing to them, the chances are you will get booked. In my experience, I typically find when booking at a new venue, the booker will put me on the calendar for one date, noting we can discuss more dates after seeing how the first gig goes. Do not push the booker on this, as doing so makes you look aggressive and desperate. It makes sense for the booker to see if you perform well in their establishment, if their clientele likes listening to you, and if they make money that night. Thank the booker for putting you on the calendar, tell him/her that you look forward to playing, and mention you will post on social media and e-mail your mailing list about the gig to let your followers know you will be playing there.

Two of these three things are just respectful signs of gratitude, indicating to the booker that you are a decent person, giving a good impression, and building a good foundation for a lasting musician-booker relationship in the future. The latter is acknowledgment you know what they are looking for when they hire live music—more people to come through the doors and increase their sales. Indicating you have a mailing list and a social media following will make a venue feel better about booking you, as it suggests they will have a decent turnout for the night even if the establishment's usual clientele is not there. It also shows you take the gig seriously and you will put forth effort ahead of time to make sure it is a successful night for both you and the venue.

UTILIZING CONNECTIONS IN A PREVIOUSLY ESTABLISHED NETWORK

Aside from cold-calling and cold marketing, another one of the main routes to booking gigs is utilizing connections you already have. If you are new to the music scene, you may not think you have many connections. You could be right, but you may be thinking about the people you know too narrowly. By only thinking about the people you know who are actively engaged in the music community, you are disregarding friends, family, and acquaintances who are not musical but may know venue owners, bookers, or employees at an establishment you want to play at.

You may be asking, "How do I find out if people I know know these people?" It's actually pretty easy; just let the people in your life know what you are doing. When talking with friends, family, and acquaintances, tell them you are trying to start performing at different venues. Give some examples of the venues you are looking to play at or the names of places you have already played. The chances are if the people you associate with are aware you are looking to gig at places they know people at, they would be happy to help you.

I have used this method a couple of times. The most fruitful connection came from a work associate of my mother's who gave me the contact information of a manager at a local chain of restaurants. I reached out to them, sending a list of the places where I've played, my genre and repertoire, a link to me performing, and of course, the name-drop of the person the manager knew. The manager booked me for a couple of gigs, and I have since gone on to perform at their establishments on numerous occasions over the past few years.

Also, don't be afraid to connect with other gigging musicians for contacts. This is something I will talk about more in depth in later chapters, but I think it is relevant enough to this chapter to discuss briefly now. In my time playing music, I have found many musicians to be rather competitive, trying to beat out other musicians for gigs to prove to themselves they are better. Yes, booking gigs is competitive to some extent, and to be successful you need to be professional, talented, and stand out from the musical pack. That said, on a local level, being cutthroat in pursuit of gigs is unflattering and will likely close more doors for you than open them. As a musician, helping other musicians get gigs is not just good because it's a kind thing to do. It can be beneficial to you in the long run, as they may be able to help you get a gig later on down the line.

However, the way you do this needs to be classy. For example, let's say you are subbing for Band A at a venue you have never played at before. At the gig, you will most likely have the opportunity to meet the booker. You should definitely introduce yourself, but you should not start making a pitch for Band B, which you are also a member of. It is professional to recognize you are at the gig as a member of Band A and should not give the appearance in front of Band A that you are trying to undermine their ability to book gigs there. While you booking a gig there in general certainly isn't inherently undermining them, they may feel threatened by more bands playing at a venue they play at. So, just because they believe booking gigs is a competition, it doesn't mean you have to as well. In order to avoid any potential drama, just get the booker's number and follow up with them a day or two later—soon enough after the gig so they don't forget who you are—and make your pitch then.

So, to offer a main takeaway for this route to gigs, be aware your friends, family, and music peers cannot help you if they do not know you are looking for help. Market yourself in your circles and tell them your performance ambitions. If they know people who can help book you somewhere, they will almost certainly help you. If they do not know anyone who can help book you and by chance meet someone who can later on, they will likely tell you about it.

Before actually going out to attempt these routes to book gigs, I recommend you do some thinking on which route(s) you plan to use. Some may work better to get you into certain places than others. Regardless, I highly recommend you attend some open mics. Even if you do not plan to use them to help you book gigs, performing at them will help you build a reputation among other local musicians and a network, which certainly won't hurt.

In the next chapter, we will be discussing venues and equipment, and what you need before performing at the gig.

CHAPTER 5

WHAT'S THE DEAL WITH THE SOUND?

―

In the summer going into my senior year of high school, I booked a gig at a restaurant located at a skiing resort. It was a reputable place, and I was excited to perform there. On the day of the gig, I packed up all my gear and drove for almost three and a half hours to the resort. Upon arrival, I found they had a whole speaker system and mixer board already there. I had packed my speakers, mixers, and cables for no reason. Granted, it didn't hurt to have the extra set of equipment on hand, but I did some pointless work.

Imagine the inverse of this situation: I just assume the venue has the equipment I need, so I don't pack anything and proceed to spend three hours driving to the venue. I walk in to discover there is no equipment there for me to use, and I do not have enough time to drive home and back to pick up my equipment. The outcome of this situation is far worse than the first, but the problem in both is I made assumptions.

In the previous chapters of this book, I have written at length about not making assumptions about your audience and their musical preferences. In this chapter, we will focus on not making assumptions regarding venues and the expectations you should have for them. This might seem obvious, but I feel it is important to note and could potentially save you from unwanted embarrassment, as exemplified in my second scenario.

If you are a musician who intends to play at bars and restaurants, as a general rule, based on my experience, you will almost always need your own sound system. In the six years I have been playing, only three restaurants had their own sound systems.

This gets into a matter of your personal finances because sound equipment can get rather expensive. As you spend more money on speakers, the better quality they will typically be. The opposite is true as well; if you spend less money on speakers, they will typically be poorer in quality. When I go out and see live music, I've seen a mix of everything. Some folks use cheap speakers, and some use really nice ones. While pricy speakers will certainly give you a more refined sound, in my opinion, what makes or breaks a live performance at the end of the day is the actual performance of the artist. Nice equipment can enhance things in small ways, but the most important thing you can do is excel at your craft if you want people to listen to you. Thus, the matter of what speakers you need is largely a personal financial decision.

However, one other thing you should consider as far as speakers are concerned is making sure they can get loud enough without distorting the sound too much. If you are playing in a smaller space, speakers that can fill a big room are not needed. A cheap pair of speakers should be able to fill a small room without much issue. However, if you are playing in a bigger space, you want to keep notice of your sound quality as you turn up the volume nob. As the nob gets turned higher, distortion will typically become noticeable, especially on cheaper models, as they distort faster with the cheaper parts they are made with. This could especially be detrimental for singers, as the distortion from cheaper speakers could prevent the audience from hearing their lyrics enunciated clearly. So, how easily a speaker distorts is definitely something I would take into consideration when purchasing speakers.

Another important piece of gear you'll need for your sound system is a mixer. There are a lot of different mixers out there with different numbers of channels you plug your speakers and instruments into. If a mixer has fewer channels, it will typically cost less than one with more channels and vice versa. There is nothing wrong with having only a few channels, but you want to make sure your mixer has enough channels for anything you'll need from it. If you are a solo artist, a mixer with only a few channels—between two to eight—is a fine purchase, as all you probably need to plug in is your mic, guitar, and two speakers. However, if you are in a band, you may need a much bigger mixer for a bigger setup. You will have multiple instruments and potentially more than one mic that needs to be plugged in. This would demand a mixer with more channels—probably twelve or sixteen.

While on this topic, I highly recommend buying a wireless mixer you can operate with your smart phone or tablet.

Oftentimes bands like to position traditional mixers off the stage behind their audience. (Granted, I do not see this done much at restaurant and bar gigs, simply because there is not much room.) Bands position the mixers behind the crowd with a person operating the board so the sound can be adjusted to an appropriate level for the audience, instead of doing guesswork with the sound from the stage. If you purchase a traditional mixer, you will need to run a snake (an extension cord to the mixer that cables plug into) from the mixer to the stage, which goes right through the audience. As a liability issue, many venues will have you tape down the snake cable so people don't trip over it. Quite frankly, I just find it to be a pain to set up. With a wireless mixer, the mixer is set up beside the band with the instruments and speakers plugged in, and then someone can walk about the audience, connect to the mixer wirelessly, and adjust the sound well. It is just way less of a hassle in my opinion, but it does come at a higher cost.

Aside from speakers and a mixer, you will obviously need your instrument and its corresponding cables. Even if the venue has a speaker system already there, the chances there will be a guitar laying around are slim to none. At every gig I play, I always abide by a rule of two (not a reference to *Star Wars*), meaning I bring two of basically everything to my gigs: two guitars, two guitar cables, two mic cables, and four speaker cables (two for each speaker in the pair). With an extra of nearly everything I need, I am ensuring I've done practically everything I can to make sure nothing can go wrong. If a guitar string breaks, I don't need to stop to restring it because I brought another guitar with me. If a cable doesn't work, it's not a problem because I have a spare.

The show must go on and having replacement gear on hand is a surefire way to make sure it does.

There are a few other pieces of equipment that may be desirable to improve your sound quality. If you are a guitarist, you will get a better sound from miking your amp or running your amp through your mixer directly, as opposed to running your guitar directly through your mixer. When playing solo, I found running my acoustic amp directly into a mixer increased the quality of my sound by leaps and bounds.

If you are in a band, something to consider, especially when you start getting more gigs in bigger spaces, would be drum mics. In smaller venues, so long as your drummer plays dynamically—having good volume control with consideration of the band and not hitting the drumheads too hard—he/she should be able to control their own volume fairly well. That said, drum mics can make the overall cohesive sound of the band a bit better, as they allow the person operating the mixer—out among or behind the audience to hear the band as the crowd does—to blend the drums with the rest of the band's instrumentation.

Moving back to the expectations you should have for venues specifically in regard to equipment, if you are an artist playing at ticketed music venues, they will typically have their own sound system—speakers, a mixer, cables, and a mic. However, unless you have been there before, there is no way to verify what they have.

So, for both musicians playing at restaurants and bars and those playing at ticketed venues, you need to know what equipment is there. I know this all sounds like common sense, but making assumptions is an easy way to not have something important on hand you need for the gig. Thus, you should either 1) contact the venue ahead of time and ask if they have any sound equipment, especially if you have never played there before, or 2) go to the venue yourself and see if they have a speaker setup.

Being prepared with your equipment is a step that can be easily overlooked and by avoiding assumptions about what equipment the venue may or may not have, you are assuring you won't embarrass yourself by lacking a cable or speaker. Lastly, have your own equipment to set up at the places that do not have any equipment there. This ensures you can perform anywhere that is willing to have you.

CHAPTER 6

WHY DOES AMBITION FEEL LIKE REJECTION?

In the fall of 2016, I recorded an inexpensive, five-track demo I planned to use to pitch myself at different venues. I got some semi-professional looking photos taken of myself and put them in the demo CD case, along with my business card. I felt legitimized by all of this. I had followed the general advice I found on music columns online and that a couple musical friends had offered me. I told myself having this professional, well put-together demo was going to get me all the gigs I wanted. It didn't.

I spent months driving to different restaurants and bars after school, dropping off my demo and giving anyone who spoke to me my pitch for why they should hire me. They all said they would give the demo a listen and call me back. None of them did. I would return a few weeks later to follow up, and they would apologize, saying they had been busy and still hadn't gotten a chance to listen to the CD. As the weeks went by, there was still no follow-up from any of them.

I had all of the ambition I felt I could ever need to succeed, but success wasn't there. Instead, all I felt was rejection. The feeling I wasn't good enough became extremely pervasive in my thoughts. It seemed every door was shut right in my face, despite having put together a professional pitch and demo. I wondered whether I should just stop trying to pursue playing live music altogether, since following all of the advice I had found or had been given was not working.

I felt defeated.

Maybe before, or even after reading this guide, you've attempted to book gigs for yourself and didn't find success. You may have invested the time to become a great musician, formulated a setlist well-aligned to the musical preferences of your ideal audience, presented a polished pitch, and offered professional-looking videos to bookers. Yet, you haven't succeeded. Further, perhaps you question whether or not you should even continue trying to enter the gigging scene.

The truth is this book will not guarantee you success. I can't promise that just because you read these pages and follow the advice within that you will be able to land gigs. These pages lay out the best practices to do so, but there are lots of factors that could prevent you from booking a gig if we're being realistic. Maybe you aren't as good as you think you are. Maybe a booker won't let you in the door because they are loyal to or satisfied with their regular rotation of performing musicians. Maybe you had a bad review or a poor testimonial on your social media. Maybe they saw an inappropriate post on your social media they don't want their venue to be associated with. Maybe they saw you at their open mic, liked your sound, but saw you were dismissive of the other musicians there and don't want to hire someone with that attitude. Maybe the bookers are just busy and haven't contacted you yet because they either forgot to follow up with you or just forgot to even watch the video clip of you playing that you gave them. There's a whole list of reasons why you may not have found success yet.

However, your reaction to not yet being able to secure a gig is perhaps what is most important. I was demoralized for a bit, and most of us probably are about something at some point in our lives. It is easy to feel defeated and become the victim of your own story. That said, should you cast the blame for not yet meeting your goals on others instead of yourself? Of course, the convenient way to cope with shortcomings is to blame others. Blaming a booker for not recognizing your talent is a way to avoid acknowledging that maybe your musicianship or pitch needs improvement. Believing musicians at open mics are conspiring against you because they don't immediately offer to help you avoids acknowledging you may not be acting very courteous toward them. In short, blaming others won't get you anywhere, and success doesn't typically come overnight. You need ambition and some level of grit to play music professionally.

I do not mean to say your blame is entirely misdirected. It could be a booker truly doesn't acknowledge your talent or your fellow musicians just don't feel like extending opportunity to you. It could be you are just acting like a victim, or maybe you do validly have people to blame. Either way, my greater point is it is not productive for you to sit around, disgruntled and moping, holding on to disdain in your heart for others, instead of embracing your ambition and continuing your efforts to book the gig.

It is hard to maintain your ambition in the face of rejection. We are all human, and we all fail sometimes. However, if you have really thought about your "music you"—knowing how motivated you are and that being able to gig is something you truly *want* to do—you won't make excuses, and you won't quit. You will be immersed in the hustle until you get the gigs you want. If people reject you, you'll get over it because your ambition will not succumb to the punches the hustle will throw at you.

On this topic of handling rejection, I spoke with Tom Snow, a locally renowned pianist, recording artist, educator, and arranger, who has been in the music business for around thirty-five years in the Greater Portland area. He has five albums to his name and performed on tour with Jonathan Edwards, who is known for his 1971 song, "Sunshine." Tom succinctly offered the insight I'm trying to convey in this chapter: "If you can't handle getting knocked down, you should probably think about doing something else." This is certainly not meant to sound jaded about the industry. It just means you need to be realistic and have some grit in pursuit of your gigs.

Furthermore, if you've invested in a music education, any setbacks you face may be even more discouraging. Let's say you've invested in a four-year, undergraduate degree with a music major. The job market is highly saturated, and you're competing for positions in only a couple career paths (assuming your degree is not in either music business or production): music teacher or performing musician. Upon graduation, you could potentially have student loans totaling around a quarter of a million dollars (assuming no financial aid at a private university), and you may find there is an overwhelming amount of competition in your job market. So, in order to make yourself stand out more, you go back to school to earn a masters or maybe even a doctorate. You may be in a financial hole of a few hundred thousand dollars at this point. What is the reward for all of your money spent? Gigs that pay between one hundred and three hundred dollars. And being realistic, if you're in the bar and restaurant scene, one hundred to one hundred fifty dollars is a much more accurate figure for a solo artist.

If you were paid one hundred fifty dollars—which is what I would consider to be decent pay for a bar and restaurant gig—every single night of the year, you would earn $54,750. And if we are being entirely honest, there is almost no way you will be able to book bar and restaurant gigs every night of the year. Thus, I have no idea how you are going to pay back your massive loans. Granted, you may make good tips, which would definitely help, but you are clearly playing a losing game. I don't write this to discourage you if music is your passion and it is what you decided to go to school for. I offer this example to demonstrate both a real situation many musicians face and how discouraging life for a musician can actually be with this much debt and an inability to book consistent, or any, gigs.

As you read this chapter, you should think back to the "music you," specifically in regard to your motivation. You need a thick skin more than anything else. You need to believe in your music. As Tom put it: "I believe in me. I believe in my songs, and I would do this anyway even if it weren't for the money. I'd still do it." You truly need that level of love and commitment to your music at the core. When the going gets rough, you need a solid motivation.

Not only do you need commitment to yourself and your music, but you also need confidence in yourself and your music. If you truly believe you have talent and you can make music people will love to hear, why should you let anyone stop you? Sure, there will always be haters, but does the average person listening to your music actually know if you're good or great? I would argue no. They don't know the skill level required to play different songs. Something super easy might sound impressive to them, and something extremely intricate and difficult may bore them. While you should certainly always try to cater your songs to your audience, it's okay to acknowledge that deep down the average person has no standing on which to judge you. Your fans can be guilty of this. They may just really like your personality and that you play covers they like or are nostalgic for. Even venue owners are guilty of this to an extent. Obviously, venues want to feature great musical talent, but at the end of the day, the priority is earning a profit from food and drinks sold and ticket sales.

Hopefully the realization some of your critics are not actually in a good enough position to criticize you makes rejection a bit easier to bear. Sometimes their criticisms are largely based on nothing but their perceptions, which may be ignorantly founded. At the end of the day, you are typically your own best critic because no one knows your music like you.

This is not to say your audience is dumb; that is obviously not what I am saying. But just to be crystal clear, I am asserting the vast majority of people who hear your music have no musical background or no idea how much time you invested into preparing a piece. However, they know the music they like; there are sounds that appeal to their ears. If they like your music, that's wonderful. Be respectful, thankful, and grateful. Although they don't know what goes into your music, they support you and appreciate you. Treat them well and you'll build a loyal audience with potential to grow.

If you're not a musician and you're just reading this for insight into the industry, please do not feel insulted. That is not my intent. This is just an acknowledgment that those who aren't actively engaged in making music themselves don't typically know what goes into the music.

Wrapping back around to handling feelings of defeat, if you hold your head up high in the face of rejection and keep hustling, you will be fine. You may not get the desired gigs right away. No one can rush success. But, if you are a true professional, in your music and in your behavior, I'd be hard-pressed to believe a booker wouldn't eventually extend you some opportunity. Just be patient, and remember not to beat yourself up too hard over criticism from those who reject or criticize you. In general, they are in no position to offer an addendum on your music. You are the artist, and it is your responsibility to decide what criticism is truly valid and/or warranted.

Believe in yourself. Believe in your songs. Believe in the music.

CHAPTER 7

HOW DO I ENGAGE MY AUDIENCE?

Have you ever had a moment where something so unexpected happened it caused you to wonder: "What the heck is going on?" When engaging with your audience, such moments can occur, and how you handle them can determine the dynamic of your relationship with your audience.

In the summer of 2016, I had one of these unexpected moments. I was playing a gig at a venue I had never played at before. It was a restaurant with a cool ski village vibe, and customers filled the spacious venue. When I started playing, I noticed I had a party of middle-aged folks seated near me who were really vibing with my performance. They liked my sound and were huge fans of my song selection.

So as not to detract from my point, I will leave what happened next up to your imagination. What a few of the tipsy women at the table did next was an unwanted, but otherwise innocent advance. While I found this advance to be a bit humorous, the shock almost derailed my performance. I nearly stopped playing because I was so thrown off guard. The only thing I could control in this situation was my reaction, which is what determines both how your audience will think of you and how the rest of the gig turns out.

I was able to play through the incident despite my shock. Then I kept myself calm and collected, laughed, and thanked them for the tips they proceeded to offer. I showed the room I had a sense of humor by being able to laugh off this uncalled-for scenario. Most importantly, my ability to make light of the situation gave me an image beyond just being a musician. When personality enters the performance, you become an entertainer. The audience, beyond liking me for my music, could now connect a personality trait they liked—a sense of humor or being easygoing—to my identity, which made them more inclined to like me. Further, by connecting to a personality trait, they may be more inclined to become fans who will come see me again.

At the time, that gig was certainly the best one I had performed. I had prepared a few solid sets the crowd loved. My performance was good, and the acoustics in the room were great. I was able to connect with the audience on a personal level. It was a standout gig, and I remembered it as such as time passed. Two years later, I was playing a gig three hours from that venue. About twenty minutes in, the party from that gig two years ago—with the women who partook in the unexpected behavior—arrived. One of the men in the party made eye contact with me, wondering if I recognized their group, and I responded with a grin and a nod. His face lit up as he started to tell the rest of his friends I remembered them.

That gig two years ago had meant something to them because they were thrilled I remembered them. Talking to them between sets, I found out they had been planning to come see me for a while and this gig two years later was the first night that worked for all of them. At that initial gig, I had earned new, big fans, but I didn't find out until a couple years later. Not only is performing a great show important, but engaging with the audience and showing them your personality can enhance your show by simply being likable.

Since that second gig, I have gone on to play multiple private gigs for this group, and I've come to know them as some of the nicest and funniest people. However, what if on that first night I played for them, I just lost my cool when the women did something so unexpected? Imagine if I had stopped playing altogether and demanded they get away from me and let me play my music. If I had gotten upset, I could have lost my hold of the room, which was amused by the tipsy women dancing around, who they saw as just having a good time. They would have seen my scolding as an overreaction. And, since the women were clearly fans of my music, they may have seen me as being unappreciative.

As a side note, if anyone ever does anything to make you feel truly uncomfortable at a gig, you are obviously entitled to ask the person to leave you alone or request the manager resolve the situation.

You may be wondering why I bring up this whole story and the adjoining hypothetical scenario, especially since I'm leaving you to imagine the unexpected act that started it all. But it's a grand example of how important it is to be prepared to react appropriately to wildly unexpected incidents, no matter how rarely they occur. It also serves as a good example for remembering to stay engaged with your audience, even if the audience behaves a bit crazily. So, let's dive into how to generally build some rapport with the audience.

If you go out to see a popular local musician, you'll typically find they have a bit to say in between their songs. If I'm being honest, I am awful at talking in between songs. It makes me uncomfortable because I usually don't have much to say; I just like to entertain people with my music. It is absolutely an area in which I need to improve. Thus, I interviewed some people who are actually very good at building a connection with their audience. When interviewing Phil Divinsky, a musician who has been gigging since 1977 and has performed across the country, and his son Lyle Divinsky, who is also an accomplished artist who has played from New York to Colorado, they both stressed how important building a relationship with one's audience is.

Lyle described the relationship between the musician and the audience in a very insightful way, saying, "The musician and the audience should be seen as a symbiotic relationship, as opposed to one versus the other." To put this in simpler terms, both the musician and the audience are really feeding off one another to create a great moment. If the audience loves the music and can connect to the artist on a personal level, they will exude engagement and energy in the moment. The artist in return will tend to perform better and offer more of his/her personality to the gig. With this symbiotic relationship, there is mutual gain between the musician and the audience, and a real personal connection can strengthen this relationship.

You're probably wondering what kinds of things you should talk about between sets. If you are playing a really popular cover—something like, "I bet you all know this next one. It's a classic from 'X artist.' Sing along if you know it."—feel free to take some liberties and add a bit of your own personality. A bit of humor always helps; people like funny people. If it is a cover of a song that isn't too well known, I would introduce the song, letting the audience know who it's by and maybe what it's about or why you like it.

When playing original music, I think talking in between songs is much easier. You just introduce your songs, offering a bit of insight into what the song is about or the story behind you writing it. Offering an inside look into your songs makes the audience feel like they're part of something special—that they're getting a sort of exclusive insider's look at your artistry.

That said, you also want to make sure you don't talk too much. You need to remember your primary purpose is to perform music. I'd say thirty seconds to a minute should be plenty of time to talk about a song. The audience wants to hear you play more than they want to hear you talk. I know this may seem like dueling advice: "here's what you should talk about" but "make sure you don't talk too much." Quite frankly, it is a bit of a balancing act. A safe rule would be to say something after every two or three tunes you play. This way, it won't give the impression to management you're just sitting around monologuing and not playing. It also makes sure you are able to engage the audience on a personal level and don't come across as too talkative and obnoxious.

There is something else you can talk about, though. Perhaps a better way of putting it would be there is *someone* you can talk about: your audience. If there are people who you can tell are really engaged already—singing along, tapping their feet, smiling, clapping, and appearing to have their full attention directed at you—feel free to make eye contact with them and ask them how they're doing. Maybe even make them feel extra special by asking them if there's a song they'd like you to play. That is certainly an effective way to win over a new fan.

Further, if people come up to you and ask you a question or offer a compliment in between sets, chat with them for a little bit. It also doesn't hurt to walk around during your breaks and initiate conversations with folks who you can tell really enjoy your music, letting them know you appreciate their listening. Tell them about yourself and your music, give them your story. Then tell them where they can find you on social media or where you'll be playing next so they can come see you again. This is an invitation for them to become a part of your story.

Moreover, there is a way you can prompt your audience to come engage with you between sets. When speaking with my friend Darren Thiboutot on the topic of audience engagement, he talked me through how he does this at a typical gig. He said the most important thing one can do to prompt audience members to come talk to you is stay visible. He always tries to stand by his equipment between sets so if anyone in the audience wants to come up and offer a compliment, ask a question, buy a CD or other merchandise, or just chat, they know where he is. You don't want to just disappear out of your audience's line of sight for too long.

Further, Darren offers some great, simple advice on making people who want to talk to you into fans, or even "super fans." This isn't a skill everyone has, but try to remember the names and faces of the people who come talk to you. If someone likes your music, knowing their name is such a huge compliment to show that person you appreciate him/her being a fan of yours. It's really simple, but it could turn someone who just likes your music into a casual fan, or a casual fan into someone who will start coming out to most of the gigs you play. It just makes your listener feel truly appreciated.

Before concluding this chapter, all of my advice about talking and engaging with your audience assumes you can tell they like you or at the very least can tell they are listening. If you are struggling to win over your audience when talking in between sets, stop talking. Just focus on playing and trying to win them over with a good sound. As Darren phrased it: "When you're up on stage, all eyes are on you. And if they're not, you just have to leave them that way. You can lead a horse to water, but you can't make it drink. But if the horse does drink, you'll notice the energy of the shows start to get better and better with the crowds getting bigger and bigger."

In conclusion, to connect to the audience you perceive yourself as appealing to according to your "music you," make a connection with them. Try chatting with them a bit between your sets and showing you appreciate them supporting you. Showing them your appreciation will—at a basic level—make you a person they want to support, not just a musician they like. I know talking to people you don't know in your audience can be intimidating, but embrace the challenge. You can do it, and it will serve your music career well to be able to talk kindly and calmly with those whom you are not already associated.

Be kind. Be appreciative. Chat a little.

CHAPTER 8

SHOULD I HAVE MAJORED IN MARKETING?

Obviously, when you book a gig, you don't want to perform for an empty room. When I booked my first gig, in the hope of gathering a following, I started a Facebook page solely for my music. For the next several years, events were literally all I posted. To some extent, that was fine. The people who followed my page and liked my music knew where and when they could hear me play. That said, I could have done more to market myself and increase the following I had.

With no knowledge about how to succeed with social media, the marketing plan I had for myself led nowhere. All of the same people came to my shows and liked my posts—mostly family and friends. I'm obviously very grateful for them and their support, but as an artist, you ideally want to see new people coming to your shows and engaging with your posts.

A successful social media marketing plan can succeed in attaining new followers if executed properly.

I openly admit marketing myself on social media is not a strength of mine. So, I thought it best to learn from someone who works daily at the intersection of business and music. Meet Jay Troop. Having a lifelong passion for music, Jay has played in multiple bands in Washington, DC, as well as in New York. He has an educational background in science and technology, currently working for Pandora and Sirius XM, analyzing musicians' data (i.e., number of plays) to gain a comprehensive and accurate understanding of where an artist really is in their career. Outside of his work life, Jay is a member of the band Harville, who notably played at the Afropunk Festival in Brooklyn.

MONEY EARNED & MONEY SPENT
Jay stressed two main components to social media strategy. The first concerns the money earned and the money spent. Not every gig will win you fans, but most should earn you money. With the money you earn from your gigs, you should allocate a portion to the promotion of your social media posts. That amount can be determined by you, and you can test the waters per se by promoting posts with different dollar amounts and seeing the interaction and reach they get.

Jay stressed to never spend more than you earn. This seems like common sense, but it is important to note. Your aim with social media marketing is to build your brand as an artist online. This goal will not be sustainable if you hemorrhage all of your earnings into promotions. The number of followers you have may increase, but you will quickly run out of money, and then your number of followers will either become stagnant or decrease.

As not all gigs will win you fans, Jay also told me a story about a gig that wasn't ideal for winning new fans and how his band leveraged it in their favor anyway. It was a corporate event, and the people were not directly focused on them; it was a business function first and foremost. Jay and his band were sort of background music. They were not making fans at this gig, but they were making more money than they would normally make since it was a private, corporate gig. So, they allocated some of the extra profit from this gig toward promoting their social media posts, thus winning them new fans later down the line.

FAN ACTIVATION

The second main component to Jay's social media strategy is fan activation—getting in front of people who are interested in hearing your music. The bulk of this is done by what we have already discussed at length about in this book: booking gigs and performing for audiences that will appreciate your music. To activate your fans, you need to engage with them. A good first step is telling people to follow your social media pages at your gigs so they will know where to see you in the future. Another effective measure is leaving out a pen and a sheet of paper by your equipment so people can put down their e-mails to be sent updates as part of an e-mail list. (Be sure to let them know you have an e-mail list they can sign up for!)

Further, let's say you get some people from a gig to follow you on social media. That's a great first step in building a following! However, what are you going to do to remind these new fans who you are and to make sure they don't forget about you? Most people who are successful on social media produce lots of content and post consistently. This may certainly seem intimidating, as content creation can seem like a second job apart from being a musician, depending on how much time and effort you put into it. Jay offers a good recommendation that will save you time with content creation: make sure to walk away from every gig with content for social media. This could be videos of you performing songs, photos from the gig, or pictures of you with audience members. As he so aptly put it: "You should look to maximize the impact of each gig."

CONTENT COLLECTION

This may seem like more work than you want to put into a gig, but if you want to grow your following, it is solid advice to follow. A way to lighten the load of collecting content at your gig would be to bring someone to the gig who will record video and take photos for you to use. This could be a family member or a friend just using their smartphone. (A high-end camera really isn't needed.) And if they'd like to be compensated for their time, you can take some money out of the budget you have for promoting social media posts.

Beyond just taking photos and video, Jay noted if his band believes a gig is important enough for them, he may even pay a stylist friend for his/her time to make sure the band is looking fashionable for the gig's photos and video. Remember, you should try to maximize the impact of each gig; activate as many fans as you can at each gig and get as much content for them to see on your social media later when they follow you.

Once you have the content, do not feel obligated to post all of it. If you feel like a recording just isn't good enough—like you messed up some notes and feel it gives a poor impression of you—don't post it. Do not be that desperate for content and, also, don't head too far down the rabbit hole of perfectionism. If you are looking for the perfect take, you may drive yourself crazy, unable to achieve your own expectations for yourself. If a recording is pretty good, I would post it. If you have a great recording, post it and put a bit of promotional money behind it by buying a Facebook or Instagram ad.

Beyond providing content for your fans and the new ones you may reach with the promotions, these posts of you performing provide a record of where you have played. They also demonstrate who you are as an artist to anyone interested in your music or any bookers who check your social media when considering to hire you. Bookers will be more inclined to book you if you have a considerable number of followers, as they perceive followers translating to audience members, and if you have video performing for an audience. If they can tell when watching the video the audience is engaged—dancing, singing, clapping along—that bodes well for you. Bookers want to hire musicians who can both bring their fans to their venue and keep them there.

INCREASING REACH
In order to reach people more effectively beyond the fans who already follow you on social media, Darren Thiboutot

of Memphis Lightning stressed the use of hashtags when he explained his social media marketing strategy to me. He told me for each gig he plays with his band, he typically designs more than one poster to post on their social media. Most of these posters have photos of the band performing live to show those who may not be familiar with the band they are reputable. Then, at the bottom of each post, he uses a few different hashtags to try and reach different groups of people, such as: #live, #livemusic, #concert, and #localmusic. By doing this, anyone who searches any of those terms may see their event and consider attending.

Also, Darren recommended tagging friends who you know will attend the event. Let's say you know ten different people who will be coming out to your show. If you tag them in your post advertising the event, each one of those ten people's friends will see it. If each one of those people is connected with five hundred people, five thousand more people just saw your post than would have otherwise.

CONSISTENT POSTING & BEING ACTIVE ON RIGHT SOCIAL MEDIA PLATFORMS

Another tip provided by Jay and corroborated by Darren was the use of posting with consistency. As mentioned, you want to get as much social media content as you can from every gig, as it lets your fans know you are active and proves to bookers you are legit. Moreover, the element of consistency is so important because it keeps you in the minds of your fans. The more content they see from you, the more apt they will be to decide to go to one of your shows. A lot of people say you need to post every day or every other day for success.

You don't need to post every day. It could be once or a couple times a week. What matters the most is it is consistent. If you decide to only post on Wednesday afternoons, make sure you are posting every week on Wednesday afternoon.

Furthermore, in order to engage your fans and potential fans, you need to decide what platforms you want to be active on. I have only ever been active on Facebook and Instagram, but those two platforms are just my preference. It is your choice as an artist to decide where and how you want to build your brand. Jay recommends that on whatever platforms you choose to use, you are comfortable and stay authentic to who you are. Social media marketing can be hard work, and maintaining your own tone and voice will make it less grueling and let your fans connect with the real you. If you like putting your thoughts out there or posting short jokes or stories, Twitter may be the optimal platform for you. If you want to share videos of you playing covers or original songs, Instagram or TikTok may be more ideal.

Beyond choosing a platform you think fits you, you also need to consider if your audience is present on those platforms. If you think your music will appeal more to a younger demographic, then you may want to be on platforms utilized more by those age groups, like TikTok. If you are aiming to reach an older audience, more activity on Facebook would be beneficial.

You don't need to be active on every platform. As I said, I am only active on two. But I would recommend one of those platforms be Facebook. This is actually for a reason unrelated to growing a following of fans. Instead, Facebook can be used in a strategy to book gigs. If you message a venue's Facebook page through Facebook Messenger and they don't respond to you, it lowers their page's response rate. In other words, if the venue chooses not to respond to you, folks who look at their page will perceive them as uninterested in engaging with customer questions, as they will see the venue has a lower response rate. So, even though the person who runs the Facebook page may not be the person who books, you will most likely at least get a response from the venue this way, and you will likely get the e-mail of the person who does the booking for live music.

PROMOTIONAL AGENCIES

All of this may seem rather intimidating. It can be a bit demanding to create so much content, especially if you decide to post consistently each day. You may face some burnout. An alternative to ease the energy required would be to work with a music marketing agency. Looking to learn a bit more about agencies and how they can benefit musicians, I spoke with Pat Timmons, one of the founders of Pop Off Agency in Boston, Massachusetts. His agency works with independent (unsigned by a record label) artists looking to grow a following and play shows. They largely focus on assisting the artist with branding and making a marketing strategy, which includes defining a brand identity, making a logo, producing merchandise, designing a neat Instagram page, and empowering the artist to be their own creative designer. With Pop Off Agency, all initial consultations are free, so if you think taking on all of the responsibility for social media marketing may be too much and you are willing to part with some money to divvy up the work involved with managing your social media, working with an agency like Pop Off may be beneficial for you.

Alternatively, while this probably isn't an option most musicians performing at bars and restaurants would pursue—but artists playing their own music at ticketed venues may—signing with a record label may be worth considering. Before his passing, I was fortunate enough to speak with Ryan Brady, an executive at Atlantic Records, which has many notable artists signed, including Charlie Puth, Coldplay, Ed Sheeran, and Sia. As I've said previously in this book, following the insights offered will not guarantee such success as that had by the aforementioned artists. I mention them in order to reflect the reputable standing of the label Ryan worked for and his standing as someone certainly knowledgeable about record labels. As far as bigger record labels go, Ryan said they offer the musician artist development resources, including a team that helps them organize tours, manages their marketing and social media, and supports them in making music the musician really believes in.

In addition to the big-name labels like Atlantic Records that probably come to mind, there are many smaller independent record labels where you likely have a better chance of being signed. These labels can offer support with music distribution and marketing, although they lack the resources of the major labels. As signing to a label is certainly several steps beyond playing bar and restaurant gigs, I would recommend it to artists playing ticketed venues with much consistent success, who are looking to build their artist brand more and move away from more local level performances.

Now that we have discussed how to market your events via social media, it is time to talk about booking gigs specifically in regards to artists playing their own original music and ticketed shows.

CHAPTER 9

WHERE CAN I PLAY MY ORIGINAL SONGS?

In June of 2017, I released an EP of original songs, titled *Waiting on an Answer*. I had CDs made and arranged for the songs to be digitally distributed. But for a while, I had no idea where I was going to host the release party, where I could perform the new songs to the public for the first time. As I've stated previously, my music career has been almost exclusively focused on cover gigs at bars and restaurants. I knew neither of those venues would be particularly appropriate for a show where I would release my songs.

Luckily, through a friend, I received a contact to a gentleman who owned a venue for weddings and other functions. He put me in contact with the booker for the venue, and we arranged a date for me to do my release show. I marketed the show online, texted family and friends to invite them to the show, ordered CDs to sell, scheduled rehearsals with the band, and printed out a blank list for folks to write their e-mails on in order to start an e-mail list. The release party had a good turnout of folks, and I made some decent money with ticket sales and CD purchases. However, as I continued to write new music, I consciously began to look for more venues where I could perform my original music.

Since I have been comfortably set in my local cover music scene and able to consistently book shows and guarantee earnings of "X" amount per gig, I ended up not pursuing the gigs for my original music as much as I had intended. COVID-19 also hindered plans to play my own music more.

I acknowledge much of the insights offered thus far in this book apply to cover gigs at bars and restaurants. So, for those readers who are intrigued most by the original music scene, this chapter is for you.

To learn more about this specific type of gigging, I spoke with several accomplished musicians, one of whom was Kris Rodgers. Kris is the singer and pianist of the rock band Kris Rodgers & The Dirty Gems, who have toured across the United States. With several albums to his name, Kris has been performing his original songs for audiences since the early 2000s.

While his perspective does link to touring, which many of you most likely are not nearly ready for yet, his initial point will serve you well to remember. That point is you almost certainly cannot play back-to-back gigs in the same general location with the expectation you can bring an audience each night. This may be a bit shocking, as you may know people who play original music who play a fair amount, but let's talk through why this is generally true.

If you book a gig at a venue for your original music one night and get all of your fans to come, why would they come to the show you booked the following night when they know it will be all of the same songs they heard the night before? In its essence, playing shows in the same general area frequently dilutes the value of your music to your fans. Your audience won't feel as inclined to come out to one of your shows if you're playing all of the time, which is a dichotomy when compared to the cover gig scene, in which musicians book all of the gigs they want without this worry.

Cover musicians can do this because people are already familiar with the songs they play, so they can win over the people who are already at the venue. Musicians playing their original songs generally need to bring their pre-established fans to the venue, since they are the only people familiar with the musicians' music.

So, if you're playing with great frequency, on one level, that's great. I'm glad you're taking every opportunity to perform and share your songs with your audience. However, you're also taking the risk fewer and fewer people will attend your shows as a consequence.

Further, while the frequency you play in a general area is significant, frequency becomes less of an issue when you're willing to travel. As a general rule, Kris recommended you aim to not play back-to-back nights at venues within forty-five minutes of each other. By following this rule, you are maximizing the frequency you can perform while also reaching a different audience segment. If you play in Town A on Friday and play in Town B on Saturday, which is an hour away, the audience who came to the first show probably wouldn't plan on coming to the Town B show since it is so far. At the Town B show, you would be playing for a different audience from the Greater Town B area.

For those doubtful of this rule, it is worth considering the perspective of venue owners. I spoke with Ken Bell, the owner at the Portland House of Music in Portland, Maine, in order to gather insight from such a perspective. He told me—while obviously any venue wants to have the best quality music and he is always looking for musicians with a lot of raw talent—the highest priority is they are able to bring people into the venue. A venue survives off of ticket sales; it is the lifeblood of a live music venue. If your bookers know you are playing just down the road the night before the date you want to play at *their* venue, they will almost definitely decline. They know your audience will see you the night before and they will not sell as many tickets when you play at their venue as a result.

Before I go any further, I think it is important to note if you don't care about selling tickets and just want to perform your own songs, you can do that. There are lots of coffee shops you can go to that are conducive to singer-songwriters. You will probably be playing for free or for tips. Alternatively, you could just have fun playing your originals at open mics and seeing how people react to them. Or—I would not recommend this—you could just book gigs at traditionally cover artist venues and play your original songs anyway, but you will generally have low turnouts and some financially poor nights, which will almost definitely result in you not being booked again. If you are alright with that, by all means, you do you. For a refresher on how to get a coffee shop gig or play at an open mic, please refer to Chapter 4, "Why Should I Go to an Open Mic Night?", as the same insights apply.

Returning to the topic of booking gigs at ticketed venues, you need to bring people to the show to sell tickets. You may be saying: Andy, if you're telling me if I want to play back-to-back nights, the venues need to be about an hour apart, then how am I supposed to have an audience at the gig out of town? Good question. One thing you could do is design a poster for the event and send it to the out-of-town venue to have them hang up on their windows. Social media marketing targeted at the town where you will be playing would also be useful. However, Kris stressed getting on the bill for another band that will be playing is the best way to get a gig at a live music venue. A band that already has a gig will make most of the decisions on the music and how the gig itself goes. Thus, they can typically pick their opening act.

"But I don't know anyone who plays in a band at the live music venue I want to play at! What am I supposed to do?" I can already hear your question, and its solution is simple: use the Internet. Search bands that play music in your genre in the area of the venue. Once you have a few, find their music on your preferred streaming platform and give it a listen to ensure your music would work well being performed before theirs.

Keelan Donovan, a Texan singer-songwriter who tours across the United States and had a song featured on the TV show *Nashville*, suggested a more specific method for finding musicians to partner up with. He recommends going to Pollstar.com and searching the city you want to play in. The website will provide you with a comprehensive list of all of the live music happening in that area. With this list, you can identify the musicians who are booked to play on the night you would like to. Find and listen to their music to make sure your music would suit theirs well. If it does, search for their social media page or website. They will typically have a phone number or e-mail available. Send them a message with a link to your own music so they can hear whether you would be a good opener. If they say no, try again with some other groups. If they say yes, you've got yourself a gig, just like that.

Hitching yourself onto the bill of another band is ideal for several reasons. First, and most obviously, it gets you into the venue you want to play at. It does this in the best way possible: putting your music in front of the people who will give it the time of day—other musicians. Second, since you're just attaching yourself to another band's gig, you don't have to worry as much about bringing people to the gig yourself. This leads to the third benefit, which is providing you with the opportunity to perform for an audience that likes your kind of music, as you and the headliner will be of the same style, which means you can build a new fanbase in a new area with the headliner's fans. This will benefit you if you return to play at this venue, as you can tell the booker or band whose bill you want to hitch yourself to you can now bring some people, assuming you are able to activate these fans (refer to Chapter 8, "Should I Have Majored in Marketing?").

While booking directly through the other musicians on the bill is definitely the most ideal way to book such a gig, this may not always be possible. In some cases, the e-mail address on the musician's website may connect you with the artist's booking agent. Alternatively, if you fail to connect with a musician, you may need to reach out to the venue directly, and you should be able to find the e-mail for booking on their website. Assume this e-mail is spammed with other people inquiring about playing there, so the chances of response are low, which is part of the reason hopping onto another band's bill is so nice.

Let's say the booker does respond to you. A booker is typically not going to be as easy to win over for adding you to a bill as the artist would be. However, the key pieces of information the booker will be interested in are whether you sound good and whether you can bring people—the latter of which is deemed more important. So, you will send them a link to your music, ideally one of you performing, and they will very likely ask how many people you can bring. Both Kris and Edgardo Cora stressed you should never give an exact number of how many people you can bring to a show. If the number you were to offer is too low, the venue is done with you. So, you tell them something like, "I filled the room at my last show" or "I bring a good crowd." You need to offer a statement that both favors you and gets around the question. Obviously, if you can't bring a fair number of people, don't lie about it. But if you think you can bring some folks to supplement the main act or bring enough people on your own, plus those from an opening act if you are the headliner, then such a statement would be appropriate to offer.

You certainly want to avoid telling the booker you can bring a specific, high number of people. If you can't deliver on that number, you will likely be blacklisted from the venue. Getting into these live music venues can be extremely competitive, so it is essential not to shoot yourself in the foot during the negotiations. If they accept this response, you should have the gig. If not, you were most likely screwed anyway because you offered a number that was too low for them.

Another final tip when messaging bookers or even bands would be to use a strictly band or artist e-mail address. Drew Zieff of the Boston folk group Jake Swamp and The Pine recommended this tactic. When his group first started trying to book gigs, they did not have much credibility, aside from their raw musical talent. They had not played many places other than open mics. So, Drew used an e-mail address he had made for the band when messaging venues and wrote in the third person. By doing this, he was able to take advantage of the appearance of being an established, self-managed artist, as the group had a specific e-mail dedicated to engaging with venues and other bands as opposed to using just a personal e-mail. Using a clearly music-specific e-mail address helps give the impression you are active enough in the music scene to need a specific e-mail for booking, and thus are more credible than some other musicians messaging venues or bands at first glance.

So, when booking gigs to play your own music, there are two main routes you can pursue: playing for free at any place that will have you, such as a coffee shop, or booking at ticketed live music venues. To book at these ticketed venues, it is most effective to do some research online and try to partner with musicians who are already booked to play at your desired venue. They will be the easiest to persuade, and if you succeed, you both get a gig and potentially new fans.

Further, repeating the process of booking gigs at different venues in different states by connecting with musicians who are playing there is how a lot of artists book their tours. Maybe you can try that once you have done enough locally to feel comfortable with both the booking process and your own live performances. Regardless, I hope this chapter offers you the insight to book the gigs you want, allowing you to share your original music with a dedicated audience.

In the next chapter, we will discuss the most underrated key to success with booking gigs: being a good person.

CHAPTER 10

SO IS THIS A COMPETITION?

You may be wondering what being kind has to do with your musical career. The simple answer is *everything*. Beyond absolving yourself of perceiving every musician you meet as a competitor, it leaves you content with who you are as a person—one who is kind to others and generous with giving others opportunities.

As I mentioned in the introduction, when I was in high school, I partook in a "Battle of the Bands" competition. I gathered some young musician friends of mine together and we started rehearsing. We wrote five original songs for the competition, making sure each song showed off each member's musical talent. We practiced for hours and hours at each rehearsal because we were determined to be the best group. Moreover, we aggressively marketed at our respective schools and amongst our friends. We were determined to show up to the competition with the largest turnout. We wanted to win.

At the first round of the competition, we had a great performance. There was definitely room for improvement, but it was very good overall. We had the largest turnout of fans too. We ended up making it to the next round. So, we began prepping for the final of the two rounds of the competition, which was in the following weeks. To be very honest, reflecting upon those weeks before the final competition, the music itself seemed to take a backseat. The motivation for our group was solely winning the competition. It wasn't a love for the songs we'd written or the fun we had playing as a group. It was about being able to say we were the best young band around.

In retrospect, I'm glad we didn't win. Our egos didn't need that. We were playing for the wrong reasons—not for the music, not even for money, but for everyone to know we were talented. We were too ambitious, seeking glory to some extent. While we were talented, we definitely were not as good as we pictured ourselves in our heads. We lost touch with the joy in making good music and viewed the bands competing against us as enemies to be beaten. We were upset the band that won would be able to book gigs more reputably than we would be able to. We became crippled with jealousy over the success of others and disbanded because of our egos.

Obviously, this period of my life is not one of my proudest. But every failure teaches a lesson, and there is an important one underlying this story that many musicians miss. When going out to open mics or just trying to book gigs in general, there can be a lot of competition, especially if you are in a big city. And, yes, sometimes you'll encounter artists who are extremely cutthroat and will speak poorly about you to others in the hopes of dwindling the number of gigs you can get. Frankly, people like that are crummy, and you shouldn't waste your time and energy worrying about them or trying to compete with them.

Instead, you should realize most of the musicians you meet and who are trying to get gigs at the same places as you are actually good people. Why would you want to make enemies out of these people by making your relationships toxic with unnecessary competition? You shouldn't. It will wear you down, thinking other musicians are trying to steal your gigs. Just be kind to them.

In fact, it is beneficial to become authentic friends with other gigging musicians. Perhaps more radically, it can be beneficial for you to refer a friendly musician to a booker at a place you already gig. "How could that be? It's one thing to be kind, but it's another thing to give up a gig!" Consider it an investment in goodwill. If you help someone else book a gig at a place they haven't played at, somewhere down the line, they may help you book a gig at a place you haven't played at. Kindness begets kindness, and generosity begets generosity. Creating healthy and beneficial relationships with other musicians is not only the ethical thing to do, but it is also an effective way to score gigs.

In application to the open mic scene, this is important. Michael Krapovicky made the point you could be the most talented musician in the world and show up regularly to an open mic night looking for gigs, but no one is going to help you get the gig if you're a jerk, treating everyone around you like an afterthought. Alternatively, if you perform well, are respectful of the other musicians' performances, and are kind to the people you talk to, the person running the open mic or other regulars who play there are more inclined to put in a good word with the booker for you.

As I mentioned in Chapter 4, "Why Should I Go to an Open Mic Night?", Mike was an early advocate for me in my music career. I had never met him until I showed up at his open mic, but I was kind to him and respectful of the other musicians there. He was kind to me in return and noted how serious I was about performing and that I was coming back week after week. He referred me to multiple gigs that gave me the "street cred" I needed to book gigs at other places. Being a nice person really did pay off for me.

Furthermore, being a nice person and building good relationships with other artists is especially important for musicians who play their own music. As discussed in Chapter 9, "Where Can I Play My Original Songs?", a good way to book gigs where you can play your original music is by connecting with other musicians who play at the venues you want to play at. If you become friendly with them, chances are they will ask you to open for them again, quite possibly at another venue at which you have never performed. Opening for your musical friends at different venues is a good way to book gigs because you can tell the booker you have played at all of these other venues. Even though your friends technically booked the gigs, you still performed at them.

Paul French, a guitarist, performing musician, and Berklee College of Music graduate, corroborates the importance of being a decent person when it comes to positive relationships with other musicians and bands. When he played lots of ticketed shows with his own bands, he would reach out to the musicians he knew weren't jerks to ask if they would perform as openers. These folks would then ask him if he would want to be on the bill at their shows.

Lastly, the other benefits of building good relationships with other musicians is it could open a spot for you in a band or as a fill-in at a gig. If X Band's singer gets sick before a gig and you have opened for them before, they may call you and ask if you can sing at the gig. There may be better singers they considered having sub for their band, but you are the one with whom they have the best relationship. They know you're nice, low-maintenance, and can do that job well. Familiarity and being kind get you the job.

Another similar scenario would be in the case of a band. A musician you are friendly with may ask you to join a new band he is starting because he knows you are talented and easy to work with from your pre-established friendship, whereas he may not know as much personality-wise about other potential candidates. Having members who are egotistical and high-maintenance is the downfall of any band, or at the very least, a formula for an unhappy band. If you can show your musical friends and acquaintances you are nice, talented, and laid-back, you will stand out as someone your musician friends will want to work with in the future.

In short, be kind to your perceived competition. They are more than likely good people trying to hustle for gigs just like you. Befriend them, help them book gigs, and they will help you down the road. Believing booking is a competition is perhaps the most draining thing you could do while trying to hustle. Support your peers and they will support you. Your music career—and your conscience—will benefit as a result.

CONCLUSION

You made it to the end!

As we conclude this journey together, let's recap some of the key lessons. Before you start hustling for gigs, you need to define the "music you"—determine what genre of music you want to play, to whom that genre appeals, and your reasons for wanting to perform live music. Further, you need to be well-rehearsed. No one will hire you if you are prone to mistakes when performing, so be honest with yourself with where you are musically and work to improve. Preparing a great repertoire of songs is also extremely important, ensuring you don't lull your audience with songs that sound too similar or songs that are too unfamiliar.

When you are finally ready to start hustling, make use of the different routes to gigs, including open mics and cold-calling. You want to be able to get yourself and your music in front of the bookers—ideally by letting them hear you live, like at an open mic—or by a recorded video you send them in a cold marketing inquiry. Once you have a gig, be sure to leverage social media marketing to your advantage, letting your fans know where you are playing. If you have a good audience turnout, the venue will almost certainly book you again for future gigs. Also, prior to the gig, you should ensure you have all of the equipment you need to fill the venue optimally with sound. And, when you are actually playing the gig, it is important to really engage with members of your audience. This is how you will build up your fanbase.

Furthermore, just be a good person. Treat your fans and the musicians you meet along your journey well. The musicians you meet are in the same boat as you, doing their best to hustle for gigs. Help each other. Do not fall into the trap of a competitive mindset. Mutual assistance is the most beneficial policy for all musicians looking for gigs. It can help you get more gigs in the long run, and it's also just a nice thing to do.

And last but not least, debatably the most important insight is to not give up the hustle when not immediately attaining success. The hustle is hard. It demands significant time and effort. If you believe in your music, keep trying, because no one else will believe in your music until you do.

For the musicians reading, I truly hope the advice and resources in this book are of value to you. More than that, I compel you to use them. Hustle, and share your music with your communities. If you have struggled to book gigs in the past, if you implement all of the lessons in this book, your odds of success with booking should certainly increase.

If you are a parent of a musician, please encourage your child to keep playing music. As you've read, this book spells out exactly how a musician can play music for money. It is a very optimal summer or part-time job for a young musician.

For those who rediscovered their passion for music or learned an instrument during the COVID-19 pandemic, when the world opens up, your communities will be excited to hear you perform. I encourage you to move from playing in your living rooms to playing on stages. Your music will be a gift for all of those looking to finally hear live music again.

Young artists will constitute the next generation of musicians. Please support them however you can—whether you are a parent, family member, friend, or acquaintance to one—and work to make your music communities more inclusive for all musicians, not just the ones who are old enough to crack open a cold one.

Musicians, please believe in your music and be excited to share it with the world. We're excited to hear it.

Thank you so much for taking the time to read this book and trusting me with advising you how best to engage in the music hustle. I appreciate it more than you know.

All the best and keep rocking!

Andy Penk

Mic Drop

ACKNOWLEDGMENTS

When I began writing *The Music Hustle: How to Book the Gig*, I had no idea how much work the project would entail. (It was a lot.) But the process was eased by the community around me, and I am truly grateful for all of your support. Fulfilling this dream of authorship would not have been possible without all of you.

Thank you first and foremost to my family for supporting me through every step of the way, always attending my gigs, and affording me the opportunities of a musical education. And thank you to my friends for both putting up with me and supporting my musical endeavors. Lastly, thank you to all of the music educators who steered me on the road to becoming a gigging musician and writing this book.

Furthermore, I'd like to specifically thank and acknowledge the following individuals for their support:

Alec Towse
Alison Hayden
Andrew Gillis

Anne Marie Poulin
Ann Dean
Anthony Marro

Ben Appel
Bethany Jewell
Brent Poulin
Charlie Largay
Christian LaMontagne
Christopher Humphrey
Connor Vaughan
Danielle Concannon
Darren Thiboutot
Darren Avery
Deb Penk
Denise Penk
Doan Winkel
Edgardo Cora
Elizabeth Chabot
Elizabeth Jerome
Eric Koester
Frank Rizzo
Gregory Penk
Isabelle Rizzo
Jim Temple
Jaimie Appel
Jared Fishburn
Jared King
Jason Paquette
Jen Marro
Jessica DiSalvatore
Joseph Murnane
Josh Medrano
Justin Hayden
Kemal Pohan
Kathleen Rizzo

Kelly Towse
Kevin Hall
Kyle Severance
Lisa Andrade
Maggie Poulin
Mara Bahmer
Mary Penk
Matthew Towse
Maureen Largay
Michael Krapovicky
Michelle Belyea
Milo Brooking
Nate Jones
Nina Eschman
Patrick Frank
Patrick McCarthy
Paul French
Paul Gore
Richard Largay
Sam Poulin
Sarah Cora
Sharon Pescetta
Teresa Chabot
Tom Snow
Tony Dean
Tony Penk
Wendi O'Donovan
William Peterson
William Towse
Zach Modzelewski

www.ingramcontent.com/pod-product-compliance
Lightning Source LLC
LaVergne TN
LVHW011843060526
838200LV00054B/4145